Ancient Peoples and Places

CELTIC
BRITAIN

General Editor

DR. GLYN DANIEL

Ancient Peoples and Places

CELTIC
BRITAIN

Nora K. Chadwick

67 PHOTOGRAPHS
27 LINE DRAWINGS
8 MAPS

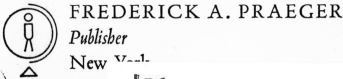

FREDERICK A. PRAEGER
Publisher
New York

THIS IS VOLUME THIRTY-FOUR IN THE SERIES
Ancient Peoples and Places
GENERAL EDITOR: DR. GLYN DANIEL

BOOKS THAT MATTER *Published in the United States of America
in 1963 by Frederick A. Praeger, Inc.,
Publisher, 64 University Place
New York 3, N.Y.
All rights reserved
© Nora K. Chadwick 1963
Library of Congress Catalog Card Number: 631–8017
Printed in Great Britain*

CONTENTS

5

ILLUSTRATIONS

To the early British bards,
our first historians

O, memorable bards, of unmixt blood, which still
Posterity shall praise for your so wondrous skill,
That in your noble songs, the long descents have kept
Of your great heroes, else in Lethe that had slept,
With theirs whose ignorant pride your labours have disdained;
How much from time, and them, how bravely have you gained!
Musician, herald, bard, thrice maist thou be renown'd,
And with three several wreaths immortally be crown'd;
Who, when to Pembroke call'd before the English king
And to thy powerful harp commanded there to sing,
Of famous Arthur told'st, and where he was interr'd;
In which those retchless times had long and blindly err'd,
And ignorance had brought the world to such a pass
As now, which scarce believes that Arthur ever was.
But when King Henry sent th'reported place to view,
He found that man of men: and what thou said'st was true.

MICHAEL DRAYTON, *Polyolbion*

THIS IS THE FIRST BOOK which has attempted to give an introduction to the history and culture of Celtic Britain between the departure of the Romans and the establishment of the Saxon kingdoms. A beginning was made when W. F. Skene published the first of his three volumes on the history of *Celtic Scotland* in 1886, and Sir John Rhŷs his *Celtic Britain* in 1884. We have travelled far since then, and it is our privilege today to carry forward the work which their genius did so much to inspire.

The proud Romans of the early centuries of our era habitually spoke of Britain as 'on the edge of the habitable globe', by which they meant outside the civilisation of the Mediterranean world. They were right. The peoples of Britain had no cursive writing and therefore no means of either acquiring Classical culture or transmitting to the late Classical world exact knowledge of their own culture. When the use of writing became familiar in the British Isles with the introduction of the Christian Church from south-eastern Europe it became possible to record the ancient traditional culture which had developed relatively independently from that of Greece and Rome—a culture which had preserved its own laws and institutions, its own forms of tradition and literature and its own moral and spiritual outlook. Thus it came about that this new art or technique of writing came to Britain from Mediterranean lands just in time to record an ancient Atlantic civilisation on the eve of our new era, and to add a final illuminated page to the manuscript of the Ancient World. It is for this reason that I have placed the chapter on the Church at the close of my book, for the Church is the link between the old and the new. Without the Church almost all our knowledge of the ancient Celtic world would have passed away; and without the Church the Celtic world would have remained for all time *in alio orbe*.

In this book I have sought to introduce the reader to some of the pleasant places of ancient Celtic Britain at the time when the Romans had left and the Anglo-Saxons had not yet penetrated in force, or established a Teutonic order widely in these Islands. It is the brief period when the Celtic peoples of Britain ruled the country, when the Celtic languages, and the Celtic customs and institutions were universal here. In spite of the fact that the Saxon ruling families and their royal dynasties, and the Saxon Laws and institutions, soon became permanently established in England and the Scottish Lowlands, it is still a fact today that in more than two-thirds of Britain the people are Celtic. The Celtic parts of Britain are by far the poorer but they are also the most beautiful, and their poverty has enabled them to retain wider vision, the timeless sense of romance and the spiritual outlook denied to the busier and more prosperous communities.

Those who knew my husband, the late Professor H. M. Chadwick, will not need to be told how much his love of Celtic Britain, and our joint exploration of the country have inspired my own researches. My debt to my former students, both Scottish and Welsh, in recent years is no less. To the fine scholarship and helpful criticism of Mrs Isobel Murray Henderson and Mr John Bannerman I am especially indebted; indeed my contacts from the Isle of Lewis to the Cornish Peninsula have been illuminating.

The need for a general book on Celtic Britain has been brought home to me forcibly by the readiness to help in every possible way which I have met from those to whom I have applied for photographs and information, especially busy officials, such as those in the Ministries of Public Works, and the curators of our national Museums. To all of these and to many others I am grateful for both help and encouragement.

Finally, in addition to the acknowledgments of photographs, etc. on p. 188 I would like to express my grateful thanks for much help generously given on a number of matters in connection with the photographs: to Mr Stewart Cruden, Inspector of Ancient Monuments for Scotland; to Mr A. H. A. Hogg of the Royal Commission on Ancient Monuments in Wales and Monmouthshire; to Mr R. B. K. Stevenson, Keeper of the National Museum of Antiquities of Scotland; and to Mr Alexander Fenton on the staff of the same museum; to Mr A. M. Cubbon, Director of the Manx Museum and National Trust; to Mr Leslie Alcock and Miss Morfydd Owen, both of the University of Wales; to Mr Charles Thomas of the University of Edinburgh; to Mr David Wilson of the British Museum; and to Mr C. A. R. Radford. My special thanks are due to Sir Ifor Williams and Professor T. J. Morgan for permission to quote their translations of Welsh poetry, and to Dr Melville Richards and Mr John Bannerman who read the proofs of my book (and made a number of corrections and suggestions); also to Professor J. M. C. Toynbee and Miss Joan Liversidge for helpful suggestions. It would be ungenerous of me were I to fail to express how much I am indebted to Mrs Rachel Bromwich's recently published book on the Welsh Triads, *Trioedd Ynys Prydein*, and to the stimulus of her friendship over many years. I am grateful to Dr Glyn Daniel and to Thames & Hudson Limited for inviting me to write this book and to Mr Eric Peters and Dr and Mrs Daniel for their constant and unsparing help without which it could never have been completed.

N. K. C.

Introduction

THE SOURCES FOR THE HISTORY of Celtic Britain
are as varied as the historical geography of the island itself.
They are found not only in our libraries, but under the earth and
all over its surface. They are eloquent in its stone and earthen
ramparts and hill-forts, its great hill-top cities and more modest
cliff castles, its shore defences, its long walls of turf and stone
and its well-defined ancient roads. They speak to us eloquently
in numerous inscriptions on stone from the Firth of Forth to the
extreme peninsulas of Wales and Cornwall, the earliest articulate messages of our ancestors; and the messages have come
down to us from several centuries and from very different social
classes and political conditions. This present book is one of a
series in which special emphasis is laid on Archaeology, the
new science which even in our own lifetime, within the span
of a single generation, has added many centuries, even mil-
lennia, to our history. We are fortunate in the possession of a
wealth of archaeological material which is now coming to light
through the most up-to-date scientific techniques to elucidate
the Britain of the ancient world.

The wealth and variety of our written sources is even greater,
and again they have come to us from several centuries, and from
the Continent, and from Ireland, as well as from our own
country, and so, naturally, in a variety of languages. We have
contemporary notices in Latin chronicles and letters and what
are virtually daily press reports by the panegyric poets of Gaul.
Only a little later are the Irish and Welsh entries in their
chronicles, chiefly in Latin, but partly in Irish, the earliest Irish
entries being often derived from contemporary poems, which
are sometimes quoted; and though the compilation of none of
the Irish annals in their present form was earlier than the seventh

century, they are derived in part from oral tradition carefully preserved by a strictly regulated professional class. For the peoples of Britain between the departure of the Romans and the establishment of the Anglo-Saxon kingdoms such oral traditions, mostly written down several centuries later, are our principal source of information.

To speak of these records and traditions of our early history as 'sources' is to do them less than justice. They are in fact, whether contemporary Latin records or even vernacular traditions, of the greatest possible interest in their own right, for in their form and style they reflect the varied phases of the civilisation and the social classes of the people who have placed them on record; the Roman officials, or the native Irish or British ecclesiastics working in an unfamiliar Latin medium; the heroic poets by their allusions in panegyrics and elegies to persons and events of whom we have no other memorials; the genealogists, who, by their knowledge of the archives—whether written or oral—of the leading families of the period, have bequeathed to us the material which might form a small Debrett of the early aristocracy who ruled Britain, first under the Romans, and later when the Romans had passed like a dream in the night.

It will not be possible in the small space at our disposal to refer to more than a few of these sources, but the reader will find it helpful to consult the brief List of Primary Authorities for the period, and the editions most readily accessible, which is given on pp. 167 f. below.

Chapter I

The End of Roman Britain

THE PEOPLES SPEAKING a Celtic language are the earliest Britons of whom we have written records. Strictly speaking the term 'Celtic' is a linguistic one, and refers to a branch of the Indo-European languages. There is no 'Celtic' race or group of tribes, or any 'Celtic' area. In general speech, however, the term has come to be used in a wider sense of the people speaking one or other of the various branches of the Celtic languages, and then, by a further extension, of their countries. This extension of meaning is a convenient one and will be adopted throughout this book.

The Celtic languages have probably been spoken in the British Isles for more than three thousand years; they were brought by newcomers, perhaps already in the Bronze Age before 1000 B.C., and reinforced in the Iron Age after 500 B.C. by a later wave of Celts, whose language in their Continental home had undergone in the interval certain sound-changes shared by Gaulish also. We generally refer to the earlier groups as 'Goedelic', the later as 'Brythonic'. The Goedelic branch of Celtic has survived down to our own time in Ireland, the Highlands and Islands of Scotland, and the Isle of Man. Brythonic has survived in Wales, Cornwall and Brittany. Scholars of the last generation believed that the Goedelic languages, entering from the Continent, were first spoken in Britain and were pushed westwards by the later Brythonic speakers, likewise entering from the Continent. Today we are asking if the Goedelic branch of Celtic did not by-pass Britain and go to Ireland direct by an early sea-route from the Continent. In any case the Irish language is believed to have been introduced into the Scottish Highlands and western Britain direct from Ireland in the early years of our era, and to have become what today we call Scottish Gaelic.[1]

In the second century A.D. the Greek geographer Ptolemy recorded the names and positions of three peoples of Britain. The Cornovii occupied the far north of Scotland, Sutherland and Caithness, and the Welsh Border in what later became Powys, with its capital at Wroxeter—the *Viroconium* of the Romans. The name is apparently preserved in the later British name of *Cornwall,* and Breton *Cornouaille.*

The Dumnonii were in southern Scotland along the Grampians, and also in Devonshire and the Cornish peninsula and part of Somerset. Their capital was *Isca Dumnoniorum* (Exeter). They are also identified with an early people of the west of Ireland known in early Irish tradition as the *Fir Domnann* ('The Dumnonii People').

The third group were the Coritani, whose native name was *Qritani,* later *Cruithni,* and who were known by fourth-century Roman and medieval writers as *Picti* ('Picts'). In Roman times the Picts were a powerful political force in the whole of Scotland north of the Antonine Wall, and as the Coritani they still occupied the north-eastern English Midlands. Ptolemy gives their towns as Leicester and Lincoln. Their language is unknown except in proper names and a number of undeciphered inscriptions, though in Scotland the royal Pictish families seem to have spoken Pictish as late as the ninth century. The Cornovii and the Dumnonii are believed to have spoken some form of Celtic; the Picts, a composite language of a form of Brythonic and an earlier indigenous language.[2]

At the time of the Roman Conquest Britain herself was divided into a large number of independent Celtic kingdoms, each ruled by its own royal house. In Scotland the kingdom or kingdoms of the Picts survived north of the Forth–Clyde isthmus; the Dumnonii in the south-west, and the kingdom or

Fig. 1. Political map of Roman Britain. The tribal boundaries are largely hypothetical (after Rivet)

'tribe' of the Votadini in the south-east. Most of the north of England belonged to the largest tribe of all, the Brigantes, but in eastern Yorkshire were the Parisii. East Anglia was in the hands of the Iceni, the Coritani still held the Midlands, the Cornovii the north Welsh Border. The remaining tribes occupied positions indicated on the map overleaf.

Fig. 1

Already *c.* 110–100 B.C. a series of movements of mixed tribes known as Belgae from France and Belgium began to enter south-eastern England, and extended their overlordship to include Hertfordshire and Essex, where the tribe of the Catuvellauni were the dominant element. From this last area the Catuvellauni extended their supremacy under their king Cunobelin in the first half of the first century A.D. over the greater part of south-eastern Britain. The Belgae now formed the most advanced element in the population, and it was they who, towards the end of the second century B.C., introduced the first native coinage into Britain on the model of the coins of Belgic Gaul.[3] This movement of the Belgae into Britain was more in the nature of an expansion than a migration or a conquest. The in-comers entered as tribal units, retaining ties with their Continental relatives, and by the time of the Roman Conquest trade relations between Britain and Gaul had been active for a long time. All the main Belgic areas had already become in part Romanised.

Fig. 1

The Roman Conquest did not change the population or the Celtic tribal units, nor the language of the people as a whole. The history of the Occupation and final withdrawal suggests that the Celtic way of life, the economy of the country, continued more or less unbroken apart from a sharp increase of civilisation in the part of the country facing the Continent in the south-east. Here towns and villas, in which Latin was spoken to some extent, were added to our map. True architecture, monumental sculpture, fresco painting, mosaic work were new arts brought from Rome, and amenities such as plumbing with a steady water supply were introduced. The official religion was Roman, first the Roman pantheon, then Christianity. But the native Celtic religion lingered on unhindered, and was even encouraged by the Romans, and fused with Roman cults; to the last, Britain remained a remote province of the Roman Empire, habitually referred to as 'a country of the setting sun, remote from our world'.

The Roman Conquest had been more like a flood than an upheaval. Caesar's two successive landings in 55 and 54 B.C. had been the first hint of the in-coming tide. The full flood tide set in in A.D. 43 with the conquest planned by Claudius. After A.D. 70 Wales had become virtually an armed outpost of the empire. The town of Caerwent, 8 miles from Caerleon, was the only major Roman civil settlement in Wales.

The revolt of the Iceni under Boudicca (Boadicea) in A.D. 61 did not stem the flood. In A.D. 71 began a northern campaign which was to extend the Roman Province over the Lowlands of Scotland. The legionary fortress of Inchtuthil, built in Perthshire under Agricola, lasted for a few years, and other Roman forts were built as far north as Kintore on the River Don; but from now onwards the waters began to ebb. Soon after A.D. 100 Roman forward aggression in Scotland came to an end. In Trajan's reign the advanced garrisons in Scotland withdrew. Scotland as a whole remained an unconquered country.

A powerful rebellion in Scotland and northern England brought the Emperor Hadrian to Britain in 122; Scotland was temporarily abandoned and the southern frontier was secured by the building of the Wall from Wallsend-on-Tyne to Bowness on the Solway. This frontier was advanced forty years later by the building of the turf wall from Forth to Clyde by Hadrian's successor, Antoninus Pius. Nevertheless, general Celtic risings in the Scottish Lowlands and the north of England in 155 and 181 destroyed the walls and almost all the forts, and in 196 a great part of Britain was overrun. The situation was recovered and the Wall and forts repaired, and in 208 Septimius Severus subdued the Caledonii of the Perthshire Highlands and the Picts of Strathmore and Strathearn in the Lowlands; but the Antonine Wall was no longer held as the northern frontier. The British tribes between the two walls were left to guard themselves and the Province against further incursions of the northern tribes, and it is a measure of their success that in the third century and especially during the fourth, civil Roman Britain enjoyed her most prosperous period—the period of the country villas and flourishing, if changed, town-life (see ch. II).

But while Britain was enjoying the halcyon peace secured by the measures of Severus and by our northern British tribes against the Picts, the Romans of the Continent were passing through a heavy ordeal. The barbarian attacks on their northern frontiers were in full swing, and Gaul was in rebellion. How long would the Romans be able to spare troops to retain her remote western province? What would be the future of the Celtic peoples of Britain if the Roman forces withdrew?

The protracted Occupation of Britain and the forty years of peace, combined with the gradual weakening of Roman power, had brought about a great change in the relations of the Celtic peoples of Britain and their Roman rulers. The British chiefs of southern Scotland were fully prepared to co-operate with the Romans to protect the northern frontiers against their mutual enemies the Picts. Also, in the late third century the relations between Roman and Briton in Wales changed radically.

About 275, serious Irish raids began in south-west Wales. An Irish dynasty and an Irish aristocracy settled in Pembroke and an Irish settlement from Leinster occupied western Caernarvonshire. Under this western pressure the Romans and the Britons of Wales found themselves no longer at enmity with one another but facing a common foe. The chief Roman defences in eastern Wales had been the legionary fortresses of

Caerleon and Chester, directed against the Welsh; part of the second legion was now transferred from Caerleon to Richborough in Kent, and a new fort was built at Cardiff against the Irish. In North Wales a fort at Holyhead, known as Caergybi, was built at this period as a protection against Irish raiders, and at Segontium (Caernarvon) at the mouth of the river a new fort was built replacing the earlier one; it was set on lower ground by the shore, in order to protect the trade of the valuable Anglesey copper mines from the same danger.[4] Nor was Morecambe Bay exempt from the raiders. At Lancaster a fort has recently been excavated, which had been built against danger from this quarter, and large forts at Piercebridge and Elslack were built to protect the area east of the Pennines from penetration by raiders from the rear.[5]

Simultaneously with the Irish encroachments on the west, serious Pictish raids were also taking place in the north. The usurper Carausius had reconditioned the fleet,[6] and his successor Constantius (293–306) had built a new fleet and carried out defences in the north and west, restoring Hadrian's Wall, and building massive new foundations at High Rochester and the great multi-angular tower at York. The great castle-like forts round the coast from Brancaster in Norfolk to Portchester in Hampshire, each garrisoned by an auxiliary regiment, and commonly known as the 'Forts of the Saxon Shore', are now thought to have been built perhaps by Carausius and Allectus to protect themselves, not, primarily, against the Saxons, but against attack from the sea by Roman authorities during the usurpation.[7] The corresponding forts against the Saxons along the French coast and on some of the islands, e.g. Alderney, were much less massive. But the great British forts were undoubtedly used later as part of the system of defences against the Saxons, when their raids in Britain began. The great activity and expert training in massive stone building occasioned by all this defence work would account for the fact that Constantius

Plates 2–5

Fig. 2

Fig. 3

seems to have supplied Gaul with masons from Britain to repair Gaulish ruined buildings, as we learn from the brilliant declamation of Eumenius of Autun in 298 on the subject of the restoration of the University of Autun.[8]

Constantius was the idol of the Gaulish panegyric poets, not only in his own day but in that of his son and successor Constantine—as well he might be. For the danger to Britain was Gaul's danger also, and on sea and land he had won for both a respite from the marauding pirates; from the powerful Pictish fleet of the far north, no less than from the daring Saxon and Frisian fleets rapidly supplanting it in southern waters. Both Vegetius in the fourth century and Gildas in the sixth speak of sea raids from the north. In an anonymous prose panegyric (formerly erroneously attributed to Eumenius), probably delivered at Trier in 297 before Constantius himself on his victorious return from his British expedition, the speaker contrasts the easy victory that Julius Caesar had when 'this people were still primitive and accustomed only to fight the Picts and the half-naked Irish'.[9]

The menace of the Saxon pirates, 'the most dangerous of all foes', is vividly brought home to us in the fifth century by a letter from Sidonius Apollinaris to his friend the Admiral Namatius, patrolling the Straits of Dover: 'If he pursues he catches . . . He has no fear of shipwreck, it merely exercises him . . . In the hope of making a surprise attack he cheerfully risks his life amid rough seas and sharp rocks.'[10]

All protective measures ultimately failed to save Roman Britain from the barbarian forces gathering strength around her borders. In a *conspiratio barbarica*[11] in 367 Irish raiders from the west, Picts from the north, and Saxons from the east simultaneously made a swift and devastating raid over a large part of the country penetrating far inland. The *dux Britanniarum*, the official in charge of the northern frontier defences, was overpowered, and the commander of the Saxon shore killed.

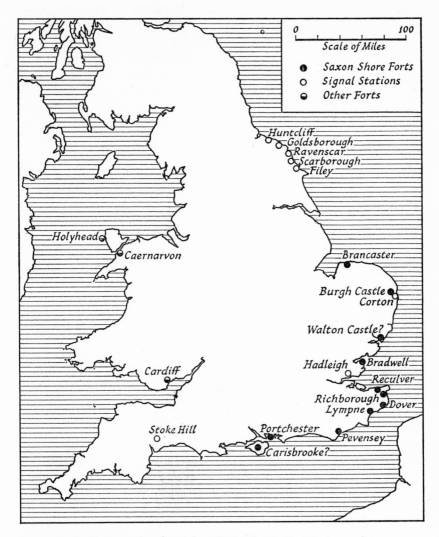

Fig. 2. The British Saxon shore forts (after *White*). *The* Notitia Dignitatum *lists nine* castella *as being under the command of the Count of the Saxon Shore. They are: Branodunum (Brancaster), Gariannonum (Burgh Castle), Othona (Bradwell), Regulbium (Reculver), Rutupiae (Richborough), Dubris (Dover), Lemanis (Lympne), Anderida (Pevensey), Portus Adurni (Portchester)*

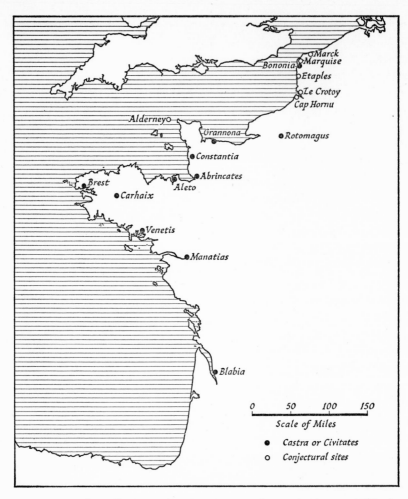

Fig. 3. The Gallic Saxon shore forts (after *White*). *The modern names of the sites marked on the map in their original Latin names are as follows:* Blaye (Blabia), *Nantes* (Manatias? Namnetibus), *Vannes* (Venetis), *Aleth or Alet at St Servan/St Malo* (Aleto), *Avranches* (Abrincates), *Coutances* (Constantia), *Port-en-Bessin* (?Grannona), *Rouen* (Rotomagus), *and Boulogne* (Bononia). Osismiis *may be* Carhaix *or* Brest, Marcis *may be* Marck, Marquise *or* Mardyck; *the headquarters of the* Praefectus classis Sambricae *at* Hornensi *may have been at Etaples, Le Crotoy or Cap Hornu*

The results to the prosperity and organisation of the country were serious for property, agriculture and commerce; but its effects must not be exaggerated. It was possible for the elaborate and wealthy pilgrimage temple at Lydney to be built during the succeeding period. Many towns such as Carlisle, York, Chester, and Leicester survived, while Verulamium also continued. The villas were not all destroyed, and in some instances, as at Langton in East Yorkshire, the damage was repaired. At East Denton in Lincolnshire an entirely new villa was built after the raid. The villa in the open country near Great Casterton in Rutland was built with a mosaic pavement and occupied for the first time in the late fourth or early fifth century—surely a sign of confidence. It is now suspected that the ultimate cessation of the villa system was due less to the insecurity of the country districts than to the general deterioration of trade owing to the disorganisation of world commerce on which they had depended.

Yet the end was gradually closing in. A brief respite was gained and security recovered by Theodosius. Hadrian's Wall was repaired, but the advanced posts were abandoned. Signal stations were set up along the Yorkshire coasts to give a warning of approaching raiding parties, but they lasted for only a brief twenty-five years before they were again destroyed by Saxon raiders in 390 and the raids continued relentlessly.

The Roman position was still further weakened by the action of Magnus Maximus, a Roman official of Spanish origin stationed in Britain, possibly either a governor or a legionary officer. His service while in Britain must have been remarkable, for the Anonymous Gaulish Chronicle states (s.a. 382) 'Maximus strenuously overcame the Picts and Scots' (i.e. the Irish); but in 383 his troops acclaimed him Emperor and crossed with him to Gaul. The nature or number of the troops which went with him is unknown. He did not remove the troops guarding the Saxon shore forts or the signal stations, and there is no clear evidence that he removed the troops from the wall.[12] His *palatini*, or personal bodyguard, are doubtless identical with the *Seguntienses*, troops referred to in the *Notitia Dignitatum* as garrisoning places in the Balkans, near Aquileia where he was killed by his rival Gratian in 388.[13]

The great General, Stilicho, arrived in 395 and reorganised the defence system, but once more withdrew the northern border to a line further south, apparently now based on York, leaving the northern British still more responsible for the defences against the Picts. And again the gratitude of the Gaulish panegyrist is eloquent contemporary testimony to the success of Stilicho's work in Britain; for in 399 or possibly 400, the poet Claudian recited his praise of Stilicho's consulship, picturing the grateful nations coming in procession to Roma's temple to give thanks for their delivery from their foes, and among them came Britain, 'clad in the skin of some Caledonian beast'.[14]

And in his poem against Eutropius he again reminds his listeners of Stilicho's work in Britain.

The Saxon is conquered and the seas are tranquil,
The Pict has been overcome (*fracto Picto*) and Britain is safe.[15]

But his confidence was grievously misplaced. We are on the eve, not only of the end of Roman Britain, but of a world crisis, and the fate of Britain is only the outer ripple of the tidal wave. In 406 a mixed body of barbarian peoples crossed the frozen Rhine, annihilating the frontier troops, and poured over Gaul. In 409 or 410 Rome, 'the mistress of the world', fell to the Goth, Alaric, and was sacked. The contemporary Anonymous Gaulish Chronicle records a specially heavy raid on Britain in the same year.

In 407 a soldier, Constantine, was acclaimed Emperor by the army in Britain, possibly against his will, and apparently by a friendly arrangement with Honorius. First taking such measures for the defence of Britain as he was able, he crossed to Gaul as Emperor, taking British troops with him to the Rhine to help the Continental army. He was subsequently defeated in battle and slain, and Procopius, our informant, adds, 'Notwithstanding this the Romans were never able to recover Britain which henceforth continued to be ruled by usurpers.'[16] Zosimus states that at this point the Britons and some of the Gauls (doubtless including the people of Armorica) seceded from Rome, took up arms, and struggling bravely on their own behalf freed themselves from the onslaughts of the barbarians.[17]

During this closing phase of the Occupation some new officials appear in the records of affairs in Britain, probably connected with the defensive measures taken on her behalf by the usurper Constantine on the eve of his departure. Here our chief guide is the *Notitia Dignitatum*. This document enables us to watch a process of devolution at work in Britain analogous in many respects to that which had already taken place on the Continent since the reform measures of the Roman Army by Diocletian (286–305) and Constantine (305–307). Briefly stated, this process entails the withdrawal and supplanting of the Roman sedentary troops massed on the frontier, known as *limitanei* (L. *limes*, a 'frontier'), by a local militia, consisting of *foederati* or federate native troops, and the simultaneous transformation of the *limitanei* into *comitatenses,* the mobile and more privileged reserves behind the *limitanei*. Naturally, transference from the ranks of the *limitanei* to those of the *comitatenses* was much coveted, and as the length of our land frontiers caused a high number of *limitanei* to be employed in Britain, an ambitious general could always offer to take them overseas and transform them into *comitatenses*.

The official in charge of the *limitanei* was the *dux*, and in Britain his was an old office functioning in the north. From the *Notitia Dignitatum* it would seem that he had sent in no recent 'returns' to the Chancellery, and this suggests that there was no longer a *dux* on the Wall, and is perhaps a further indication of the substitution of native British *foederati* for Roman troops on the northern frontiers, following the system already adopted on the Continent.

A second Roman official of some importance who appears about this time is the *comes littoris Saxonici*, 'The Count of the Saxon shore', who is believed to have been responsible for the manning and provisioning of the Saxon shore forts, each of which was garrisoned by an auxiliary regiment. The title first

Plate 6

occurs in the *Notitia Dignitatum* (*Occidentalis* XXVIII). We have no reference to any official as *comes,* 'Count', in Britain before the mention by Ammianus Marcellinus (XXVII, viii, 1) of a *comes maritimi tractus* in connection with the great raid of 367; but the title appears later among a small group created by Constantine (407–411) as part of his defence measures for Britain before he left.[18]

If the 'Saxon Shore' defences were in existence at an earlier date they must have been under another command, which may have been wider, and included the forts and fleets on both sides of the Channel. Carausius seems to have held a command on the Gaulish side of the coast before his usurpation. At some later period the Gaulish forts may have been transferred to a wider command extending along the whole coast; but the history of the Gaulish fleet at this time is very obscure, and excavation of the forts is badly needed. For practical purposes the Saxon Shore troops would count as *limitanei.* They might thus come gradually under native command; but no doubt this would be at a late stage.

The most interesting and the most obscure of these new officials is the *comes Britanniarum,* or *Britanniae,* who appears at this time in the *Notitia Dignitatum* (*Occidentalis* I, v and viii), and whose office is believed to be quite a new creation, perhaps the command of a mobile field army mainly of cavalry, but partly of infantry units. It may have been built up of such remnants of the *limitanei* of the *dux* of the north, and of the *comes littoris Saxonici* of east and south, as did not accompany Constantine to the Continent.[19]

In 410 came the famous rescript of Honorius, informing the cities in Britain that they may look after themselves.[20] This has been variously interpreted, but coinciding as the date does with the fall of Rome, there can be little doubt that it is simply an official rescind of the Roman law prohibiting barbarians from bearing arms. What, then, is the date of the end of Roman Britain? Perhaps the question is hardly a valid one, for we have been following, not a single crisis, nor even an event or series of events, but an ordered process. The *Notitia Dignitatum* enables us to watch the gradual transformation of Roman military organisation and of Roman frontier defences into native British organisation and defences. As to when the process was completed, opinions have varied by as much as fifty years. The late Martin Charlesworth[21] held that the military end came in 407 with the removal of the troops by Constantine, but that the civil administration went on till 418, the time of the council of the Seven Provinces at Arles. A date of *c.* 415 is favoured by most recent scholars, with possibly a brief re-occupation in a very limited area in the south-east.[22]

According to the doubtful testimony of Gildas (ch. 20), the Britons sent a letter to the Roman Consul Aetius in his third consulship, which fell in 466, expressing 'the groans of the Britons', and their sufferings under the depredations of the Picts and Scots. But no help came. By the middle of the fifth century the four centuries of the Roman Occupation had passed like a dream. From the time when the last Roman ferry weighed anchor, carrying the last of her troops to Gaul, till the foundation of the Saxon kingdoms in the sixth and seventh centuries and the spread of the Saxon conquests to the Highland line and the Welsh Border, to the Tay and the Severn, the whole of Britain was governed by her native Celtic princes.

c

It was in this period of freedom between the Roman and the Saxon Occupations that the ideals and the literature took shape which still characterise the Celtic peoples wherever the Celtic languages are spoken.

CHAPTER II

Celtic Rule in Britain

NATIVE CELTIC LIFE had continued unbroken
throughout the period of Roman rule in Britain, and
we can watch its emergence during the closing years, and
after the final departure of the Roman troops. Our evidence is
perhaps fullest and clearest in the survival of the heathen Celtic
religion. The most striking example of the survival of a native
cult is that of the temple of Lydney,[1] built on a precipitous
site on the right bank of the Severn. Here, some time after 364,
probably even after the Great Raid of 367, an elaborate temple
was founded and dedicated to the god Nodens, or Nodons.
The temple was apparently therapeutic, perhaps Aesculapian
in character, and on the site were also offices, cells for the
patients, and guest quarters for visitors. The buildings and coin
hoards, the mosaics, the votive tablets and offerings, including
a splendid little bronze wolf-hound, suggests that this elaborate   Plate 7
establishment was for wealthy patrons. One of the inscriptions
in a tessellated pavement, now destroyed, interpreted as stating
that an officer in charge of the supply depôt of the fleet laid the
pavement out of money offerings,[2] is an interesting indication
that there was still an official in charge of a naval depot in the
Bristol Channel. The three dedicatory inscriptions give clear
evidence of a close rapprochement with the native population,
for there can be practically no doubt that the wealthy god
Nodens is identical with the Irish god Núadu (Argatlám),
'Nuadu of the Silver Hand', and the Welsh Lludd Llau
Ereint. The temple seems to have survived until the fifth
century; but the quality of the repairs and the barbaric coinage
of the latest phase are signs of decadence, and the substantial
enclosing wall, now for the first time erected round the precincts,
is an ominous witness to the unsettled times.

The temple at Lydney had been constructed within the limits of an Iron Age hill-fort; and in the native hill-top city of Maiden Castle near Dorchester in Dorset another late Roman sanctuary had been built after 364, a simple building on the Romano-Celtic plan. We know of other examples of such late Roman temples built and richly furnished at a time when Christianity was making rapid headway in town and country, and it is thought that they may have been prompted by a heathen reaction, probably under the influence of Julian the Apostate.

The Roman type of sanctuary in Britain, as in Gaul, was a high square building surrounded by a portico, the actual architectural features being of Roman inspiration. At Silchester all the temples are of this Romano-native type and are decorated in Roman fashion. Even at Verulamium one of the oldest and most important temples was built on the characteristically Romano-Celtic, as opposed to the Mediterranean, plan.[3]

Plate 1
Fig. 4

These temples, local in style, are not the only indications of the flourishing condition of Celtic religion under the Romans. The splendid group of round, steep-sided barrows at Bartlow in East Anglia, with their rich Roman furnishings, still stand proud witnesses to the wealth and importance of the British high aristocrats under Roman rule. On a humbler plane many wayside shrines have been found with Celtic associations in a Roman context, and Celtic spring and river gods are known from Roman sculpture and river names.

In recent years the importance of the evidence of continuity is coming to be more fully recognised. Over and over again we find, in both temples and municipal buildings, that as the Roman buildings deteriorated in the late fourth and fifth centuries, repairs were effected, inferior in workmanship, and even new buildings were constantly erected on the ruins. In Verulamium the evidence of continuity is particularly interesting. Here, for example, a house built well after the middle of the fourth century had been enlarged later and furnished

Fig. 4. An impression of two of the Bartlow barrows (cf. Plate 1)

with lavish mosaics, and changes continued to be made in the structure down to 410. Still later, at least until 450, the technical skill necessary to maintain the city's aqueduct and to install a piped water supply was still available, and the civilised needs implicit in such a demand were still continuing.[4]

Intellectual continuity is no less clear. In the fifth century the Pelagian heresy was especially prevalent in Britain, 'the home of its birth', so we learn from Prosper of Aquitaine. Education was to some extent flourishing. A series of anonymous letters,[5] still extant, are believed to have been written by a Briton travelling abroad to his father, a bishop in Britain, in which reference is made to the education of boys, suggestive of the Roman high school system similar to that on the Continent. If we can rely on the evidence of St Patrick's *Confessio*—and the fifth-century date of the text is not in doubt—the Orders of the Christian Church, bishop, presbyter, deacon, were still observed even in the west of Britain. The stone funerary inscriptions of the fifth and sixth centuries show that Latin was still understood and used for formal purposes. The quality of the lettering has not yet seriously deteriorated.

The Romano-British fusion, which had been achieved through the long period when Britain formed part of the Roman Empire, and the continuity of British native life were the basis on which Britain now had to build up her independent existence from within, and to resist disintegration and conquest from without. Henceforth the Celtic peoples of Britain were compelled to fall back on their native resources. The first need was to carry on some form of civil government for internal administration; the second, to look to her defences.

Britain had been divided by Severus into two provinces, distinguished as Upper and Lower Britain, though the nature of the division is not quite clear.[6] Central and south-eastern Britain had contained most of the villas, chiefly occupied by native Romanised Britons, and also most of the towns, the important centres of civil administration. But into the Roman administrative system the earlier Celtic kingdoms, the tribal areas, had been absorbed almost intact, and each had its own tribal centre, its *civitas*, as in Gaul.

Commercial towns, such as London, and the *coloniae*, originally Roman civic urban settlements of retired troops, each doubtless had its *ordo* or permanent executive body. It seems clear that certain of these native *civitates,* or what we may call 'city states', had now become sufficiently Romanised to be able to carry on a form of organised civil life for some time, and a few at least of the *civitates* are known to have persisted.

Northern and western Britain were in general far less Romanised. In Wales, with the exception of the Silures, with their capital at Caerwent (*Venta Silurum*), we know of no self-governing system; but inscriptions to a *cives* of Venedotia ('a citizen of Gwynedd'), an *ordous* of north-central Wales, and a *magistratus* of Penmachno in Caernarvonshire,[7] warn us against an incautious generalisation from negative evidence.

It is evident that the Celtic peoples were not caught unready for defensive measures against external aggression. The Gaulish poet Claudian had been right in summing up the chief peril of Britain as arising from the fact that her enemies were now seeking entry on three fronts, the Irish in the west, the Picts in the north, the Saxons in the east. So far none had succeeded in invading on a large scale. The strong Pictish kingdoms were still contained north of the Antonine Wall by the British kingdoms stretching in a long unbroken arc from the Firth of Forth to Land's End. The North British princes would have no more wish than had the Romans to be conquered by their old enemies the Picts; and in the west the Welsh would be as concerned as the Romans had been to foil Irish attempts at penetration.

Owing to the careful preservation of the Celtic pedigrees, the North British princes, now left in control of the northern defences, are no strangers to us.[8] They were represented in the fifth century by at least three important families. Of these the great Strathclyde dynasty with its stronghold at Dumbarton guarded the western end of the Antonine Wall and counted among its chief members a certain Ceredig *Gwledig*,[9] a term of high distinction, probably the Coroticus reproached in St Patrick's famous *Letter* for carrying off some of his converts into slavery. His immediate ancestors bear names which look like corruptions of Roman names, and before them come three which have distinctly Pictish features. This would carry us back to a period shortly after the great raid of 369, and suggests that first, Pictish chiefs, and later, Romanised Britons had been employed to guard the western end of the Northern Wall as a result of the raid.

Plate 8

Bede implies the strength of the old British kingdom of Dumbarton ('*Dún Breatann*') when he refers to it (*H.E.* I, 1) as a *munissima civitas* ('a very strongly fortified *civitas*') down to his own day.

The family of Ceredig is the best known branch of a number of dynasties of south-western Scotland who trace their ancestry to a certain Dufnwal Hen, and whose family epithet is *Hael*. A tombstone at Yarrowkirk in Selkirkshire, once, like the Catstone, included in an extensive Christian cemetery, bears an inscription commemorating 'the most famous princes Nudus and Dumnogenus, two sons of Liberalis'.[10] *Liberalis* is the Latin translation of *Hael*, 'munificent', 'wealthy'. These people had no coinage or organised trade. Can the wealth of the family have originated in Roman subsidies to enable them to defend their fort and the west of the Northern Wall? Did Ceredig and his soldiers find it convenient to support the family epithet by slave raiding and slave trading when Roman finances broke down? The silver treasure of the coeval kingdom on Traprain Law, at the eastern end of this Wall, was perhaps looted from Gaul under the same conditions.

Plate 9

Plates 27, 28

The eastern counterpart of the kingdom of Ceredig in Strathclyde was Manau Gododdin around the head of the Firth of Forth. The name *Gododdin* (earlier *Guotodin*) seems to preserve that of the old tribe of the *Votadini*, which in Roman times stretched from Forth to Tweed.[11] Nennius, making use of a much earlier written northern source, records a story of a chief named Cunedag (modern Welsh Cunedda) who migrated from this region to North Wales with eight of his nine sons, leaving the eldest behind in Manau, and adds that they 'drove out the Irish with immense slaughter'. According to Welsh genealogies, Cunedag's immediate forbears, like Ceredig's, bore Roman names for three generations, and his grandfather bears the epithet *peis rut*, 'the man with the red cloak'.[12] Before these the names are Pictish, while his own name and those of his sons are normal British names. This family, like that of Ceredig, apparently grew to importance in Roman times, probably guarding in their turn the eastern end of the Northern Wall against the Picts.

Another North British prince, a certain Coel Hen, founded one of the three great families ruling and founding dynasties on the northern border before the end of the fourth, and during the fifth and sixth centuries. These we shall meet later, fighting valiantly against the Anglian invaders in the sixth and seventh centuries.

Evidence for the defences of western Britain follows a similar pattern. In the *Notitia Dignitatum* no entries whatever appear for any western frontier garrisons south of Lancashire. Had the Welsh Border defences, like those of the Scottish Border, been entrusted to native local princes? The evidence of their genealogies and of stone inscriptions suggest that this was so.

In the first place, we have the well-known Christian tombstone in Carmarthenshire which bears in Latin lettering the inscription *Memoria Voteporigis protictoris,* and in addition in the native Celtic alphabet, known as *ogam,* the Irish form of the name, *Votecorigas.* The epithet *protector* was given in the later days of the Empire to barbarian princes honoured with *foederati* status as 'protectors' of the frontiers on behalf of the Romans. There is little doubt that *Voteporius* is identical with prince *Vorteporius,* the 'tyrant of Demetia' (*Dyfed,* Pembrokeshire) censured by Gildas in the sixth century among the rulers of Britain (cf. p. 42 below).

Plate 10

The title *protector* is applied to early members of the family of Magnus Maximus on the royal genealogy of Pembrokeshire. But the early steps on these Pembroke genealogies are too vague and corrupt to merit acceptance. They carry back the ancestry of (Magnus) Maximus to Constantine the Great, and are of course inadmissible. They probably owe their origin to the desire of a descendant of Rhodri Mawr of Gwynedd (cf. pp. 73 f. below) to trace his ancestry to a famous Roman General of Gwynedd. An alternative genealogy of the ruling family of Pembrokeshire,[13] believed on doubtful evidence to date from the third century A.D., derives the dynasty from an Irish prince

Eochaid Allmuir ('Eochaid from overseas'). Here, then, we have rival traditions, one Romano-British, one Irish, for the rulers of the kingdom of Pembrokeshire, the home of Voteporius *Protector*; and the title *Protector*, applied to members of the family of Maximus, suggests that his functions may have been comparable with those of Voteporius, 'Protector' of Dyfed. His two immediate forbears also bear Latin names, and these three generations are the first which agree in all our three versions of the Pembroke genealogy. We are hardly left in doubt that the Romans had given their support to an Irish family on the south-western frontier of Wales to protect an area, already bi-lingual and largely Irish in population, against further Irish encroachments—in fact the old story. And indeed Maximus in his Roman fortress in Caernarvon, whatever his precise title, must have had this function also.

The protecting functions of those in charge of the western peninsulas of Wales is comparable with those of Ceredig Gwledic[14] and of Cunedag, guarding the northern frontiers against Picts and perhaps Frisians entering by way of the Firth of Forth, later known as the 'Frisian Sea'. Again, reference may be made to the story of the settlement of Cunedag and his sons in the maritime regions of North Wales to rid her of Irish settlers (p. 40 above). The Welsh pattern of federate protection probably helps to explain why the *Notitia Dignitatum* has no entries of forts or officials in the west. Here, however, still more momentous developments are recorded which changed the entire course of British history. At this point we leave all contact with Roman officials and titles, and henceforth we depend solely on British evidence, recorded for the most part in Latin, from oral tradition.

In the first half of the sixth century the author of the *De Excidio Britanniae*, whom we, in common with historians generally, will call Gildas, tells us of a powerful British ruler whom he refers to as a *superbus tyrannus*, and whom he evidently regards as responsible for the Saxon invasion and occupation of Britain.[15] No name is given to him in the oldest and best text, but Bede, in his *Chronica Majora*, calls him *Vertigernus*, a form which he must have obtained from an early British source, whether Gildas or another. In Anglo-Saxon the form given to the name is *Wyrtgeorn*, and in later writers it appears as *Vortigern*, generally regarded as a proper name, though it means literally 'overlord' and may originally have been a title. In the Latin of this period the word *tyrannus* (lit. 'tyrant') generally signifies a usurper, and this is doubtless what Procopius implies when he speaks of Britain as largely in the hands of 'tyrants' after the departure of the Romans. A correct translation today of the *superbus tyrannus* would be 'absolute dictator'. In much later sources, Irish and British, Vortigern is styled *rex Brittanorum*.

Here again, this great Border prince is preceded on his genealogy by three generations of Romanised forbears, and his great-grandfather bears the eponymous name of *Gloui* (apparently from Gloucester), to which is added the epithet *Gwalltir*, 'of the long hair', perhaps from the long horse-hair of the Roman soldiers' helmets. Gildas tells us that at that time all the councillors, together with the supreme dictator (*omnes consiliarii cum superbo tyranno*) invited the formidable (*ferocissimi*) Saxons into the country. This places the responsibility for the invitation not so much on the *superbus tyrannus* as on the *consiliarii*, who were probably the governors of the 'city states', with the *tyrannus* at their head. Moreover, Gildas makes it quite clear that the Saxons were officially invited in as mercenaries to fight on behalf of the Britons. The invitation was in accordance with recognised practice, and Vortigern's action was a perfectly constitutional one. The story suggests that no anarchy followed the withdrawal of the Romans.

Who Vortigern was we do not precisely know, but he is the leading figure of the fifth century in most of our traditions of the west and the Welsh Border. His ancestral territory was probably in south central Wales, for the medieval territory of *Gwerthrynion* contains his name, and according to Nennius the later kings of Buellt (Buillt) and Gwerthrynion (in modern Brecknock and Radnorshire) traced their descent from Pascent, his third son, this territory having been bestowed on him after Vortigern's death by Ambrosius, 'who was king among all the flocks (*greges*) of the British nation'. According to an early reading made by Edward Lhuyd in 1696 of the pillar of Eliseg in the Vale of Llangollen,[16] the kings of northern Powys traced their ancestry to a marriage of Vortigern with Sevira, the daughter of Magnus Maximus; but doubt has recently been cast on this reading.[17]

In later traditions, both British and Anglo-Saxon, Vortigern's power seems to have extended as far as Kent, and may indeed have included the whole of the Roman province. But he is never represented as fighting, or called *gwledig* or *dux*, or even *protector*, and Nennius tells us (ch. 43 ff.) that his army was commanded by his son Guorthemir. Our traditions on the whole suggest a Roman provincial governor, such as a *vicarius*, possibly the last provincial governor of Roman Britain. A large body of unfavourable legends gradually collected round his name, and he was universally execrated for his part in the *adventus Saxonum*; but these legends are obviously derived from saga recorded and cultivated in a hostile *milieu*, such as the fantastic account given by Nennius, writing nearly four centuries later, of his encounter with St Germanus. The same source tells us that he died *non cum laude*, and records three variant versions of his death. What seems clear, however, is that there was in fact a powerful Romano-British prince of the western border who played a leading part in the official entry of the Saxons into our history on a nation-wide scale.

In the passage of the *De Excidio* immediately following the invitation to the Saxons and their later devastation, Gildas states (ch. 25) that a remnant took up arms and challenged their victors to battle under the leadership of a certain Ambrosius Aurelianus, a *vir modestus*, and a *dux*, whom he describes as 'almost the last of the Romans', and whose parents had worn the purple and had been killed in the Saxon invasions. Their descendants, with this single exception, had greatly degenerated from their ancestral nobleness. From now on, Gildas continues, sometimes the people were victorious, sometimes the enemy, till the last great slaughter of the Saxons in the year of the siege (*obsessio*) of Mount Badon, recorded in the *Cambrian Annals* for 516.

Elsewhere (ch. 28 f.) Gildas attacks by name five British princes who appear to have been his own contemporaries, and rulers of wide territories on the western seaboard; as they are apparently his seniors his picture is in some measure that of the closing years of the fifth century. He addresses them apparently in geographical order, beginning with Constantine, 'tyrant' of Dumnonia (the Devon-Cornwall peninsula), whom he calls *Catulus*. Then comes Aurelius *Caninus*, whose order in the list—to say nothing of the juxtaposition of 'cat' and 'dog' —suggests that his location is in south-east Wales. Next comes Vorteporius, seemingly of Pembrokeshire, followed by Cuneglasus, probably the *Cinlas* of west Wales, great-grandson of Cunedag, and finally Maglocunus, the great *Maelgwn Gwynedd*, also a great-grandson of Cunedag, and the ruler of North Wales and Anglesey. Gildas's survey has covered the western coastal kingdoms of Britain, from Devon and Cornwall to Lancashire, and would probably link up with the wide north-western kingdom of Rheged (cf. p. 63 below). These wide western kingdoms had probably served as the bulwarks of Britain against Irish encroachment.

In chapter 42 of the *Historia Brittonum*, Nennius records stories of a certain *Emreis* (*l.* Ambrosius) with the epithet *Guletic*, who is victorious over Vortigern in a contest of magic in the neighbourhood of Snowdon. Emreis claims to be the son of a Roman consul, and Vortigern is here stated to bestow on him a citadel [18] and all the western side of Britain, while he himself moved northwards. In ch. 31 we had been told that Vortigern had been beset by fear of Ambrosius (*timor Ambrosii*), and after Vortigern's death Ambrosius bestows the regions of Gwerthrynion and Buellt on his third son, Pascent. This is not history, but these traditions suggest a picture of Ambrosius as a Romanised ruler in south-western Britain opposed to Vortigern, and engaged, as pictured by Gildas himself, in trying to maintain Roman authority against the invading Saxons.

If among the degenerate members of the family of Ambrosius Aurelianus there is one who was identical with any of the princes abused by Gildas, the most likely would be Aurelius Caninus. He is the only one of the five princes who has not been located with reasonable probability, and according to the order which Gildas appears to be following, his position would be in south-east Wales. The proper names increase the probability that they are identical. Neither *Aurelius* nor *Aurelianus* is a type of name found in early Welsh.

Some have sought to identify Ambrosius with King Arthur, who on various grounds is thought to have flourished in the late fifth century. The evidence for a historical Arthur is, one may say at the outset, at least highly unsatisfactory. He left no descendants, and we have no trustworthy genealogy of him, and no contemporary records whatever. Cumulatively the amount of tradition cannot be ignored. Professor Jackson concludes the most recent study of the subject: 'There may have been a supreme British commander of genius in the late fifth century who bore the Roman-derived name of Arthur.'[19] But let us be candid: there is no reliable evidence that he held any sub-Roman office, despite the statement of Nennius (ch. 56) that he was *dux bellorum*; and no evidence whatever that he was the head of a mobile field force, or acted as *comes Britanniarum*; or owed his military success to Roman military tactics or horsemanship.

Neither Gildas nor Bede mentions him, and such evidence as we possess from later sources is not calculated to inspire confidence. His name occurs in the unsatisfactory Pembrokeshire genealogies, as well as in a later version by Geoffrey of Monmouth. He is mentioned in the *Annales Cambriae* for 516 as the successful leader of the British at *Bellum Badonis*—a statement supported by Nennius; and again in annal 537 where it is stated that Arthur and Medraut (the *Modred* of later tradition) fell at the battle of Camlann. These two notices are of unknown derivation.

Our longest account of Arthur is that of Nennius. He tells us in ch. 56 that when the Saxon leaders were gaining ground in Britain, Arthur—who has not been previously mentioned— was accustomed to fight against them along with the kings of the Britons. But the twelve victorious battles [20] here credited to him are likely to have been of originally independent origin, for such lists were a common oral convention. The last battle mentioned, however, that of Badonicus Mons, has at least the support of the *Annales Cambriae*.

Much later tradition, represented by Geoffrey of Monmouth, connects Arthur with the royal line of the princes of Devon, naming one, Uther Pendragon, as his father; and poetical tradition perhaps lends some support to this.[21] Geoffrey further represents him as son of Custennin (Constantine), prince of Devon, and brings him into connection with prince Gereint of the same kingdom, and this is in line with later literary and hagiographical tradition; but on the whole none of this late tradition can be accepted as valid as it stands. The most that one can say with confidence is that there was probably a Celtic chief called Arthur, who met his death in battle against the Saxons. It may perhaps be added that St Columba's biographer Adamnán, writing before 704, records an Arthur among the sons of St Columba's king, Aedán mac Gabráin, a king of Argyll, whose family has other Welsh connections; and Adamnán states that this Arthur was killed in battle in south-eastern Scotland against enemies who included the Miathi and Saxons. He is mentioned by Adamnán (I, ix) as first among the sons of Aedán who, had he lived, would have been his successor.

However we view the historicity of Arthur, a growing body of opinion now regards his traditions as originating in North Britain, and believes that this limited Cycle of Arthur moved southwards, along with a vast body of North British traditions, such as those of Myrddin (Merlin) and other heroes of the sixth and seventh centuries, to be freshly localised in Wales and Cornwall. A line in the North British corpus of poems known as the *Gododdin* (cf. pp. 103 ff. below), probably dating from *c.* 600, refers to Arthur as representing the highest standard of valour. While this may be a later interpolation, it is one of the most convincing pieces of evidence, if not for a historical Arthur, at least for a lively North British tradition of an Arthur who was at this early date the standard pattern of a great hero and valorous man. If we could get behind the massive superstructure which southern Celtic tradition of later times has erected round a prince of Britain who perished in battle against her enemies, the present writer is of the opinion that we might regard him as a member of the ruling dynasty of Argyll, which seems to have had strong British ties by intermarriage.

Separation from the Continent has given to the British Isles its personality, and a continuity which has survived invasions and occupations. These are the great incidents of our history, but they do not give a balanced picture of the part that the sea has played in the normal life of the country; and in recent years archaeology has completely revolutionised our ideas of the earliest Saxon settlements. The evidence of the Saxon cemeteries and the pottery which they contain suggests that the Saxons had perhaps been granted settlement rights, and had been brought into the country as *foederati* long before 400, and more than half a century before the traditional date of the *Adventus*; and that even at the end of the third century Saxon settlements here were *en rapport* with both their Continental neighbours and with the Romans in this country. Whatever the explanation of the precise nature of this early Saxon peaceful life in an unequivocally Roman context in eastern Britain, early Saxon communications were evidently taking place normally across the North Sea.[22]

In the fifth and sixth centuries Britain became the centre of a large-scale maritime activity in which she herself took an important share. The Irish Sea and the waterways to the north appear in our traditions as a busy intersection of sea-routes, the northward extremity of the Atlantic coastal route of prehistoric times. The Celtic peoples were essentially habitual seafarers, with simple but fully adequate sea-going vessels, known as *curachs*,[23] *scaphae, naves longae,* etc.; and throughout the historical period the narrow and stormy seas between north-eastern Ireland and south-western Scotland were traversed constantly, while the Irish Sea, a great land-locked lake, has been, more than the land areas, the true unit of Celtic civilisation. We have seen that the Irish expansion on to the west coast of Wales had already been extensive in the Roman period, and from the fourth century onwards reached a pressure second only to that of the Teutonic peoples on the east and south of Britain, so that Irish immigrants of the fourth century A.D. may have been welcomed by friends and relatives.[24] Tradition, inscriptions, archaeology and place-names alike place it beyond doubt that continuous Irish settlement was taking place in the Cornish peninsula, along the shores of the

Severn Sea, and in South and West Wales to the Caernarvon-shire peninsula,[25] and that it had even made its influence felt in Brecon (cf. p. 69 below).

Under these conditions it is in no way surprising that in the fifth and sixth centuries, and indeed doubtless even earlier, a migration from south-western Britain into Armorica, the westernmost peninsula of Roman Gaul, established a British- (Welsh- and Cornish-) speaking population overseas, the nucleus of modern Britanny, and our first colony.[26] The reason is generally believed to have been the westward progress of the Saxons, chiefly on the authority of Gildas, who in ch. 25 refers to his countrymen being forced to leave their native land; and though he never mentions the name there can be no doubt that he has Armorica in mind. But the Irish en-croachments on the west must have offered a far stronger motive for the colonists to leave home than the attacks of the Saxons on the east. The majority of the immigrants appear on linguistic evidence to have come from Cornwall, while literary tradition hints that the leaders came from Wales, far from the areas as yet affected by hostile Saxons. Moreover, the contacts between Armorica and Britain were not new. Caesar tells us that the Veneti, the most powerful of the Armorican tribes, were perfectly familiar with the sea-routes, having a large fleet with which they were accustomed to sail to Britain.

The Britons seem to have moved into the north and west of Armorica with little opposition—on the whole a peaceful penetration. Consistent traditions suggest that the true pioneers of the migration were British ecclesiastics, who negotiated the establishment and rights with the legal authorities. They no doubt attended to the religious needs of the new colonies, but there is no suggestion of missionary activities. Indeed, the Armoricans were members of the Roman Church in Gaul. The ecclesiastics seem to have been generally members of the princely families of east Wales, Cardiganshire, and the Severn

Valley, and perhaps of Brecon. In some traditions princely leaders accompanied and supported the priests, and then became the rulers of the new colony.

An interesting glimpse of the seafaring activities of the Celtic people of this period is a little Celtic settlement and the establishment of a Celtic Church and monastery in Galicia. The early history of this settlement in north-west Spain is unknown. The area is an ancient Celtic one, in which the Teutonic tribe of the Severi had established themselves early in the Migration Period. Even after its destruction by the Arian Visigoths in 585 it retained much of its independence, and as it was a Catholic state its monasticism remained conservative. In particular the Celtic monastery of Santa Maria de Bretoña near Mondonhedo, included in the episcopate of Britonia in a list dating from Suevic times, must have been a link forged with the Celtic world to the north. The Celtic signature of their first bishop is attested as *Mailoc*. Was this little church and monastery a new creation, in response to a stimulus from Celtic lands in the Age of the Saints? Was it an Irish or a British one, founded direct, or from Brittany itself? None of Mailoc's successors can be clearly identified by their names as Celtic. The problem remains. It may be added, however, that Orosius speaks already in the early fifth century of a city in Galicia which he calls *Brigantia*, and which he regards as having some kind of relations with Ireland.

CHAPTER III

The Foundation of the Kingdom of Scotland

Fig. 5

Plate 11

Figs. 6, 7

Fig. 9

THE OUTLINE of the early history of Scotland is a particularly difficult one to trace owing to the fact that at the dawn of the period of our contemporary written records, from at least as far back as the early seventh century, Scotland was divided among four peoples, differing widely from one another in origin, and all speaking different languages. Of these the Picts of the north and east are the most archaic, both in language and institutions, while the kingdom of Dálriada (Argyll) in the west had been occupied by a branch of the dynasty ruling at Dunseverick in Dálriada in Co. Antrim as late as the fifth century. The Britons had occupied, at least from Roman times, the whole of the south, between the two walls. By the mid sixth century a new Teutonic dynasty had superimposed itself in the north-eastern territory of Roman Britain, founding the Anglian kingdom of Bryneich (Bernicia), and this new political element rapidly extended its authority up south-eastern Scotland, annexing the British area of Manau Guotodin and the whole of the old area of the Votadini.

Before the foundation of the kingdom of Dálriada (Argyll) all Scotland north of the Antonine Wall as well as the Hebrides and the Northern Isles had been ruled by the Picts, and apart from Argyll the Picts continued to be the rulers till the ninth century. Their language, which has survived only in proper names and undeciphered inscriptions, is probably a mixture of an indigenous non-Indo-European language and some form of Celtic akin to British (later Welsh).[1] They are commonly called *Picti*[2] by Latin writers, but their native general name was *Cruithni*.

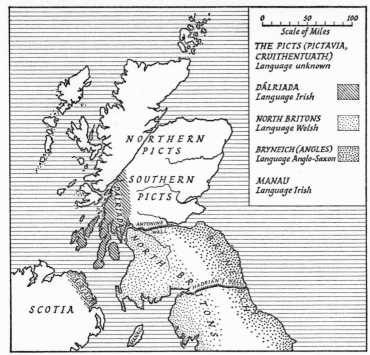

Fig. 5. *Early Scotland. The Four Kingdoms*

Bede, writing in the early eighth century, speaks (*H.E.* III, iv) of the Picts as a whole as divided into two main bodies, the Northern and the Southern Picts, separated by 'steep and rugged mountains', and the chief land communication must always have been through the Pass of Drumochter, described in a medieval itinerary as *'passagium pessimum sine cibo'*. Throughout the historical period the Southern Picts occupied the valleys of the Tay and the Earn, and appear in our records as divided into four provinces:

1. Athfotla (Atholl), the old kingdom of the Caledonii with their capital at Dunkeld ('The *dún* or fortress of the *Caledonii*'), dominated by Mount Schiehallion ('The *shee*, or supernatural hill, of the *Caledonians*'), perhaps their sanctuary. During the Pictish historical period their capital was at Scone.

Fig. 9

Plate 12

Plate 13

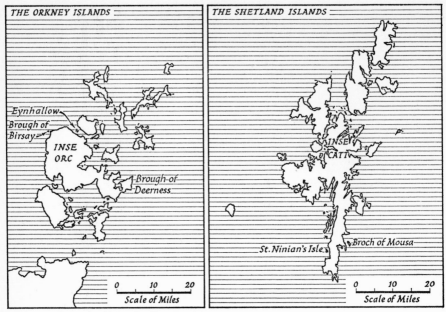

Fig. 6. Early Scotland (the Islands). The Tribes

2. Circinn or Girginn, i.e. Forfar or Angus and Kincardine or the Mearns, largely the fertile Strathmore, the lower valley of the Tay, with its capital at Forfar near the foot of Turin Hill, known today as *Dunnechain* '(the *dun* of Nechtain'; see p. 64 below).

3. Forthriu or Fortrenn on the upper waters of the Earn and the Forth, an important through route to Dálriada.

4. Fib (Fife), with its seaboard capital at Kilrymont (the 'Cell' or early religious monastic foundation of the 'royal hill'), today St Andrews.

It is possible that in the sixth century the chief Pictish power was in the north, where St Columba visited King Brude mac Maelchon[3] whom Bede calls *rex potentissimus*;[4] but as one stands today on the great Iron Age hill-fort of Castle Law above Abernethy and surveys the line of hill-forts to the north, the whole valley of the Tay comes into view as a nucleated

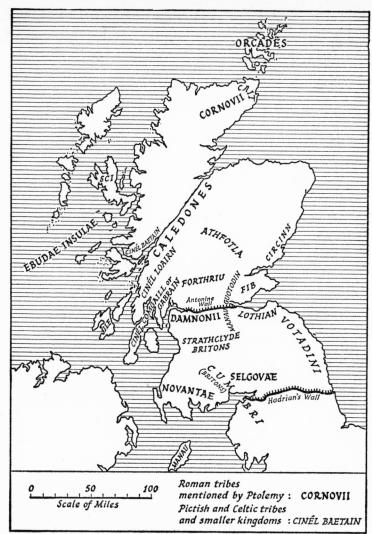

Fig. 7. *Early Scotland (the Mainland). The Tribes*

area, surely always the heart of Pictavia. And when in 685 King Ecgfrith of Northumbria struck at the heart of Pictish power under its king, Brude mac Bile, it was at Forfar that he was slain. From the sixth century onwards the struggle for

Fig. 8. Sea-horse,
Pictish symbol
stone engraving
(after Diack)

supremacy between the Picts of the north and south, and of both with the kingdom of Dálriada, forms the recurring and the most important theme in the history of Scotland till the union of the two peoples in the middle of the ninth century; and with the union, the beginning of what we mean today by the country of Scotland. A subordinate but important theme, running like a thread through the struggle during the whole period, is the relations, now friendly, now hostile, between the kingdom of Dálriada and the Britons of southern Scotland. Meanwhile the Bernicians of Northumbria were gradually extending northwards, and also making heavy inroads into these British kingdoms, till finally halted in the north by Ecgfrith's defeat and death.

All indications bear out our traditions of the Picts as a powerful nation. Some two dozen Pictish inscriptions exist, and their distribution covers the north and east of Scotland and corresponds closely with that of Pictish art represented by the 'symbol stones' to be described later. With two or three exceptions, in which the inscriptions are written in Latin letters, the Pictish inscriptions are written in the native Celtic *ogam* alphabet, and have not been deciphered; but they are believed to be late, and mostly to be assignable to the eighth and ninth centuries.[5] Thus, while they confirm our impression of the high material culture and coherent political organisation of the Picts, they tell us nothing of their history.

At some period before the embassy from Nechtan IV, king of Angus, to Abbot Ceolfrith of Monkwearmouth in the year 710, the Picts evidently had a class of ecclesiastics who could read and write. It is uncertain at what precise period the Picts as a whole became literate. We have occasional references to statements said to occur 'in the ancient documents of the Picts'[6] (*in veteribus Pictorum libris*), but this probably merely refers to lists in calendars kept in Pictish churches. A number of versions have survived of what is commonly referred to by

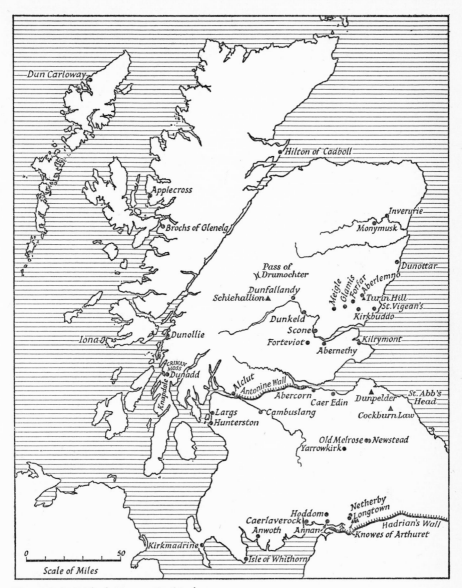

Dun Carloway

Hilton of Cadboll

Applecross

Inverurie
Monymusk

Brochs of Glenelg

Pass of
Drumochter
Dunfallandy
Schiehallion▲

Dunollie

Iona

CRINAN
MOSS
Dunadd

Knapdale

Dunkeld
Scone
Forteviot

Meigle
Glamis
Forfar
Aberlemno
Turin.Hill
St.Vigean's
Kirkbuddo

Dunottar

Abernethy

Kilrymont

Alclut
Antonine Wall
Abercorn
Cambuslang

Largs
Hunterston

Caer Edin

Dunpelder▲

Cockburn Law▲

St.Abb's
Head

Old Melrose ●● Newstead
Yarrowkirk

Netherby
Longtown
Hoddom
Caerlaverock
Anwoth   Annan
Hadrian's Wall
Knowes of Arthuret

Kirkmadrine

Isle of Whithorn

0   50
Scale of Miles

Fig. 9. Early Scotland. Sites mentioned in the text

57

modern historians as a 'Pictish Chronicle',[7] but these contain little more than lists of early kings, sometimes with brief notes attached. These lists are, in their early stages, manifestly the product of antiquarian speculation, and are wholly unreliable,[8] while the notes are often later additions to the texts, and equally untrustworthy.

On the other hand, from about 550, when close contact was established with the literate kingdom of Dálriada, the names in the Pictish king-lists are evidently genuine, for most of the names are recorded in the Irish annals and other historical works. This impression is strengthened by the fact that the names of the fathers of these kings are recorded in the Pictish king-lists, and by the actual unfamiliarity of many of the kings' names. Among the Picts succession was through the female, and so the introduction of the fathers' names is probably a late intrusive feature in the succession. The traditions of the Picts suggest that the fathers were often, if not usually, members of unrelated clans, sometimes foreign princes on a visit.[9]

We are in a stronger position to trace the outline of the history of the Scottish kingdom of Dálriada.[10] In the first place our sources from neighbouring peoples are much fuller, for Dálriada faced the western seaboard which carried a busy traffic throughout our period between the Celtic countries on its borders. Some of these Celtic areas, moreover, had been literate from the sixth and possibly the fifth century, and, though the Irish Chronicles in their present form are later, Irish annals throughout our period and down to *c*. 750 serve as a useful check on Scottish events, especially the events of Dálriada. Furthermore, the Scottish kingdom of Dálriada had kept a short Chronicle,[11] probably on the island of Iona, from the seventh century at the latest. This probably consisted originally of nothing more than brief notes added in the margin of an ecclesiastical calendar whose primary purpose was to indicate

Fig. 10

Fig. 10. Modern native Irish curachs, Blasket Island, Co. Kerry (after Mason)

the reckoning of the proper dating of Easter; but it developed ultimately into a Chronicle which may, indeed, in its early stage, have itself served as a basis for entries in the Irish annals. Dálriada being of Irish origin and character, it is quite natural that the Irish annalists regarded it as one of their own kingdoms.

The Scottish king-lists[12] trace, first the line of the kings of Dálriada, and later the kings of the united Picts and Scots— i.e. Scotland as a whole—from Erc, the founder of the dynasty in the fifth century, down to the time of Malcolm III (d. 1095), or later. Thus all the Scottish kings are derived from a common ancestor, Fergus mac Erc.[13] The earliest part of the list is made up of the so-called *Chronicle of Dálriada*. Its source is unknown, but there was a 'Scottish' king-list in Ireland in the eleventh century, containing the lengths of the kings' reigns. This is now lost, but there are other Irish historical works of the period which show the Irish well informed about the early Scottish kings.[14]

A still extant general survey,[15] probably drawn up in the seventh or eighth century, enumerates the general muster of sea and land available in Dálriada. It incorporates a brief narrative giving some details of the arrival of the sons of Erc from the kingdom of Dálriada in Ireland. The fleet carried 150 men, and was led by three brothers, Fergus, Loarn, and Aengus. Little is known of Loarn, but his family, referred to as the *Cinél Loarne* ('the kindred of Loarn') occupied the northern part of present-day Argyll with their seat on the site of Dunolly Castle at Oban, a site well placed for communication with

Plate 14

59

Plate 17

Ireland. The family of Aengus occupied Islay, and of the descendants of Fergus, Gabrán had Kintyre and Knapdale, with his chief stronghold on the rock of Dunadd surrounded by Crinan Moss. The families of Loarn and Gabrán played the chief part in Dálriadic politics, and for many years were rivals for supreme power. The eventual rise of the Cinél Gabráin to pre-eminence in Dálriada is doubtless due to the political sagacity of St Columba, who was the chief man in the power politics of the sixth century and who eventually 'ordained' (*ordinavit*) Aedán as king of the Cinél Gabráin in succession to his cousin. Aedán has left his impression on history as Dálriada's greatest king. He remained loyal to Columba till the end of his life, and it was undoubtedly their joint statesmanship which guided the destiny of this little Irish-speaking colony in Argyll until it amalgamated ultimately with the Pictish kingdom of Scotland. Already in 628 the Irish annals speak of his son and successor, Eochaid Buide, as *rex Pictorum*.

Meanwhile the kingdom of Dálriada was gradually penetrating eastwards into the territories of the Southern Picts, and towards the middle of the eighth century came to a clash with Angus mac Fergus, the most powerful of the Pictish kings. It was probably about this time that the Scots penetrated into Atholl and Fife.[16] The period 780–840 is obscure, as the Irish annals, hitherto our chief guide to Dálriadic history, fail us at this point; but it must have been one of the most momentous periods in Scottish history, for we are on the eve of the union of the Picts and Scots. The actual union was completed under the Dálriadic king, Kenneth mac Alpin, who died in 858. In all probability it came about as a gradual process, largely through intermarriage, for after 781 the Dálriadic kings generally bear Pictish names, and there is no hint of a Pictish conquest to account for this. The Pictish law of inheritance through the female doubtless greatly facilitated a union of the two peoples by intermarriage.

It is not known whether Kenneth obtained the Pictish throne by any right of succession, or by conquest. The view reflected in later chronicles is that it was by conquest. The Chronicle of the united Picts and Scots,[17] which dates from the tenth century, states that Kenneth ruled Pictavia happily for sixteen years after he had 'wiped them out' (*delevit*). Other texts also speak of a *destructio* of the Picts; but it is remarkable that no hint of such a conquest is given by records in Irish, British or English. The Irish annals, in recording Kenneth's death in 858, call him 'king of the Picts', and the title remained in use by the Irish and even the Welsh annalists till the time of his grandson. But the actual subjects of Kenneth himself and of his successors are referred to as 'Scots', and the Picts soon came to be thought of as a people of the past.

From now onwards Dálriada loses its importance. The centre of power shifts from the west of Scotland to the east, and the Scottish element in the aristocracy becomes dominant. The Dálriadic kings now live and rule in the old Pictish kingdom, and henceforth the chief royal seat is at Scone on the lovely bank of the Tay a short walk above Perth. The mound in the grounds just behind Scone Palace still marks the site of the traditional dwelling of the Pictish kings.

The British kingdom of the part of Scotland south of the Antonine Wall,[18] the immediate neighbours of both the Dálriadic Scots of the west and the Picts of the east, had emerged as a result of the withdrawal of the Romans from the northern defences. They developed in the fifth and sixth centuries under independent native princes, their territory corresponding with that of the tribes whom they succeeded. Their function had been throughout the centuries, and still remained, that of defending the territories of the Britons from alien aggression. Those in the east, in succession to the Votadini, stretched southwards from the Forth to the Tyne, and were known as the

Gododdin, keeping the old name *Votadini* in a 'Welsh' form. Those in the west, known as the Strathclyde Britons and the *Cymry* (the older form was *Cumbroges*, 'fellow countrymen', 'Cumbrians') stretched from the Clyde probably to the borders of Mercia and even North Wales, and included Elfet (modern *Elmet*) near Leeds, till the conquest of Elfet by King Edwin of southern Northumbria, probably before 616. The Welsh of Wales recognised them as close kin and spoke of them familiarly in later records as the *Gwŷr y Gogledd* ('The Men of the North', that is to say, 'Our northern neighbours').

These northern Britons were Christians and literate, but they have left no written records apart from a few stone inscriptions. Some annals or notes were evidently kept in the seventh century, and have been incorporated by Nennius into his *History* of the *Britons*,[19] but no independent annals have survived in their own right. On the other hand each British court had its official bard responsible for composing panegyric and elegiac poetry to enhance the reputations of the chiefs and to celebrate their part in contemporary events, and also to preserve and perhaps transmit the genealogies.[20] All of these constitute a highly important source for our knowledge of the period, for these oral traditions were carefully preserved by the bards and eventually written down in the ninth century, not however in the North, but in Wales.[21]

Many of the North British families can be identified from their genealogies. The most authentic is the dynasty of Ceredig Gwledig of Dumbarton in Strathclyde (cf. p. 40 above), and in the sixth and early seventh centuries their chief king was Rhydderch Hael ('wealthy'), sometimes also called *Hen* ('old'), who is referred to in Adamnán's *Life of St Columba* as *Rodercus filius Tothail*. He seems to have been reigning before the saint's death, and also as a contemporary of Aedán mac Gabráin; he is famous too in traditions of both St Kentigern and the prophet Myrddin (Merlin).

The most important of the princes of Cumbria was Urien of Rheged, with his chief centre doubtless at Carlisle, and his territory the coast-lands of the Solway and Morecambe Bay. Nennius tells us that he was the greatest war-leader whom the British had, and his family is both the most prominent and the most distinguished in the traditions of the North, both military and ecclesiastical.

It will be seen that the British territories stretched in a long unbroken arc from Edinburgh to the Welsh Border and indeed on to Land's End, and its double frontier made it a particularly difficult territory to defend. On the west were the encroaching Irish; on the north their ancient enemies, the powerful and warlike Picts; on the east, the dauntless Anglo-Saxons. The only chance of survival would have been solid unity among themselves, and a far-sighted policy of union with one of their more powerful neighbours in the North. At first, under the leadership of Urien, they were strong enough to take the initiative against the invaders from the east. Nennius (ch. 63), deriving his information from the seventh-century written records referred to above, tells us that Urien with three other British princes—Rhydderch, Gwallauc, and Morcant—fought against Hussa, king of Bernicia (i.e. the northern part of later Northumbria); also that Theodric, apparently a successor of Hussa, with his sons fought bravely against Urien, yet Urien besieged them for three days and nights in the island of Metcaud (Lindisfarne), but was murdered by Morcant out of envy (*invidia*).

Plate 15

After this early brilliant campaign against the invading Anglo-Saxons and the murder of Urien, the Britons were never able to form alliances effectively among themselves. The picture which their traditions reflect is that of a number of inchoate small states, with little conception of political stability, in fact what we have come to call a 'heroic' society. The most famous of their battles, celebrated in Welsh poetry and recorded in the Welsh Annals in 573, was the Battle of Armterid (modern Arthuret),[22] near Longtown on the Solway, 'fought for a lark's nest', as a Welsh Triad has it,[23] between Gwenddoleu, one of these British princes, and his own cousins, Gwrgi and Peredur. The *'lark's nest'* is perhaps Caerlaverock (the *caer* or fort of the *laverock* or lark), an important strategic harbour in early times commanding the approaches to the Solway on the northern bank. The Welsh poems claim that the poet and prophet Myrddin (Merlin) lost his wits when his lord Gwenddoleu was slain, and that he afterwards lived the life of a wild man in the Forest of Celyddon (Caledonia) in Scotland.

We possess a splendid collection of poetry from the next generation commemorating a disastrous expedition of the men of Manau Gododdin into Northumbria, and their battle against the Angles, probably near Catterick in Yorkshire, in which they were annihilated to a man; but after the murder of Urien the history of the Men of the North is in general that of a rearguard movement. From the sixth century, the Angles gradually extended their territory up the whole of south-eastern Scotland, and by the beginning of the seventh this area was under their king Aethelfrith. The western British kingdoms remained independent till a much later date, and the Anglian spread westwards has left no records of severe military actions; moreover, the marriage between King Oswy of Northumbria and Riemmelth, certainly a Briton, and probably the grand-daughter of Urien, suggests that Rheged came into Anglian hands by peaceful negotiation. Strathclyde remained independent for centuries, and the northward extension of the Angles was checked when Oswy's son Ecgfrith met his death at Forfar in his thrust into southern Pictland in 685. It was, nevertheless, this gradual extension of Anglian territory northwards and westwards that ultimately created the Scottish Lowlands with the introduction of the English tongue.

CHAPTER IV

The Foundation of the Kingdom of Wales

W E WOULD GLADLY KNOW more of the relations of the Britons of the North with the Britons of Wales. In the Welsh poem *Armes Prydein*[1] ('The Prophecy of Britain'), probably composed early in the ninth century, the *Gwyr Gogled* (l. 15), 'the Men of the North', are distinguished from the *Gwyr Deheu* (l. 78), 'the Men of the South', i.e. the Welsh of Wales. The terms probably originated in the North Welsh kingdom of Gwynedd, and imply a close unity between the Britons of southern Scotland and those of Wales. The term *Deheubarth*[2] (from Latin *dextralis pars*) is used of the south of Wales proper by Asser in his *Life of King Alfred* (ch. 80), and also by later writers.

Fig. 11

The natural route from Cumbria to North Wales must always have been by the Irish Sea. A story is told in an early North Welsh version of the Laws of visits by the Men of the North across Morecambe Bay to Gwynedd, and a famous medieval bard, Hywel ap Owain (d. 1170), prince of Gwynedd, claims to have ridden from North Wales to Rheged —possibly in one day:

Today I love the open north land loathed by England . . .
I mounted my bay steed and from Maelienydd[3]
To the land of Rheged I rode both night and day.[4]

It is true that in Roman times Manchester, Ribchester, and Carlisle were connected by road; but unless this route was kept open, communication from the North through Lancashire must have become impracticable for large bodies of men, even light bodies of horsemen. All the rivers flow from east to west,

E

and are not easily fordable in their lower courses. Moorland covered large tracts of country, such as Rossendale Forest in the medieval parish of Whalley in the north, while lakes such as Martin's Mere in the centre, and bog such as Chat Moss in the south, and forest—Macclesfield, Delamere, or Mondrum—offered serious obstacles to transit throughout the route. We may suspect that the early Saxon place-names in Lancashire represent settlements from the east of the Pennines rather than an organised network of communications in the west.

Welsh history is generally believed to begin with the arrival of a certain Cunedag (later Welsh *Cunedda*) and his sons, as related by Nennius in the *Historia Brittonum* (ch. 62, cf. p. 40 above). This account tells us that Cunedag and eight of his sons and one grandson came from Manau Guotodin 146 years before the reign of Maelgwn, prince of Gwynedd (cf. p. 45 above), in the time of his great-grandfather, and that they had 'expelled the Irish for ever from those lands'. The form of the name Cunedag and the context of the story indicate that the story is not later than the seventh century.[5] In one text of the royal genealogies appended to the *Historia* a list of Cunedag's sons is given in a tenth-century orthography, and at the conclusion the eldest son Typiaun is said to have died in Manau Guotodin and his son Meriaun to have divided his share of the Welsh inheritance with his brothers:[6] 'This is their boundary, from the River Dee to the River Teifi, and they held very many districts in the western parts of Britain.' There is no hint of a migration or of any large-scale movement from Manau, and Cunedag is never referred to as *rex*, or, for that matter, by any title.

There is nothing inherently impossible in the early tradition of the movement of Cunedag and his sons into Wales, as Nennius claims, save their expulsion of the Irish, which was certainly not completed so early. Elsewhere also he states (ch. 14) that they drove the Irish out of Dyfed, Gower, and Kid-

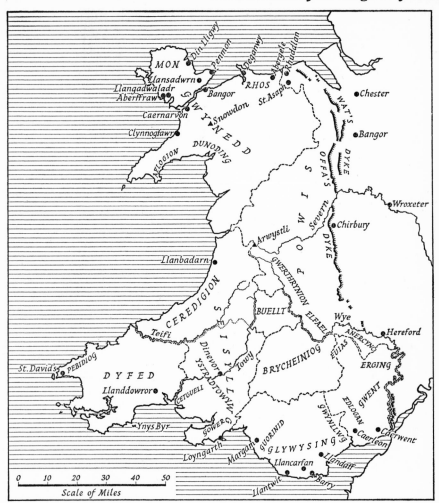

Fig. 11. Wales in the seventh and eighth centuries (after *Rees*)

wely, but there is no authority in the genealogies for sons of
Cunedag south of Cardigan, and the statement is generally
discredited.[7] In any case the additional tradition which gives
the names of the sons may well be later in origin, and merely a

piece of antiquarian speculation based on the names of the later divisions of the north and west of Wales, with which they are identical. The list is arbitrary and has gaps, and not all the kingdoms are on the coast or where Irish concentration might be looked for, e.g. Anglesey. The early text represented by Nennius makes no claim to these identifications, which have doubtless been supplied from the later pedigrees claiming to trace the origins of the ruling princes to the sons of Cunedag. All Welsh genealogies come to a halt at the close of the Roman period, and the story fills a gap. The names of the sons are possibly based on some old mnemonic list, like that of Arthur's battles. This concentration of genealogies on a fifth-century ancestor is closely analogous to those of the kings of Ireland, where the systematic scheme is attributed to medieval antiquarianism. Similar antiquarian speculative schemes were created for the sons of Erc in Dálriada, and for the sons of the eponymous Cruithne among the Picts.

Welsh tradition, then, presents us with the political map of Wales at the close of the Roman period as a mosaic of little kingdoms, each ruled by its own dynasty, each represented by its own carefully preserved genealogy, and each inheriting from father to son. Five of these genealogies claim that the dynasty which it represents was descended from Cunedag, of which four belonged to Gwynedd and a fifth to Ceredigion (Cardigan). By no means all the Welsh dynasties claimed descent from Cunedag. Dyfed (which included the modern Pembrokeshire) in the south-west kept the name of the pre-Roman kingdom *Demetia*, and was ruled by a dynasty which lasted from the fifth to the tenth century and claimed to be of Irish origin (cf. pp. 41 f. above). It has always had a special interest for us because here in the valley of Hodnant was the church of Mynyw, the monastic foundation, and later the cathedral, dedicated to St David, or Dewi Sant, the patron saint of Wales.

The little mountain kingdom of Brycheiniog (Brecknock) in south central Wales was never conquered, and its dynasty, which claimed descent from a native princess and an Irishman, lasted till the tenth century.[8] The royal line of Builth on the upper Wye claimed descent from Vortigern, and the claim was never disputed. According to Nennius (ch. 48) both Builth and Gwerthrynion (a name derived from an older form of Vortigern) were, when he was writing, ruled by Fernmail, and it is certain that the early chieftains of Gwerthrynion, like those of Builth, traced their descent from Vortigern. The kingdoms of south-eastern Wales claimed to be derived from the Roman province of the Silures, and to have a dynasty descended from Caratacus. This was always the most Romanised part of Wales, and the name *Caerwent* has survived from the ancient tribal centre, *Venta (Silurum)*.

The kingdom of Powys—beautiful, fertile Powys, 'the Paradise of Wales' as the Llywarch Hen poet calls it—doubtless arose from the old kingdom of the Cornovii, with its capital at Viroconium (Wroxeter) and its sentinel the Wrekin. It was always the gateway to Wales and had to guard its fords jealously. The name of the ford of Rhyd-y-Groes ('Ford of the Cross') at Buttington on the Severn, a few miles north of Welshpool, is reminiscent of the great medieval abbey ruin of Strata Marcella also close by the Severn, and the entire setting is immortalised in the medieval Welsh story of the *Dream of Rhonabwy* as Arthur's camp during his negotiations with the Saxons. The origin of the Powys dynasty is obscure (cf. pp. 42 f. above), but the death of Cyngen, the last king of the old native line, is entered in the *Annales Cambriae* for 852.

As we trace the separate dynasties of these little independent Welsh kingdoms from their origin in the fifth century to the gradual unification of Wales in the ninth and tenth and their final union with England under Athelstan, we cannot fail to be impressed by their stability, for they remained intact for many centuries. Some of the ruling families had a life of more than eight hundred years, and the eventual unification of the country seems to have been brought about by inter-marriage rather than by armed conflict.

The leading dynasty in the history of Wales from the fifth to the ninth century is descended from Maelgwn Gwynedd, whose ancestry traces him to Cunedag in the fourth generation, and who is to be identified with the *Maglocunus*, the 'Island Dragon' of Gildas. Maglocunus had won high approval from Gildas by spending some time in youth in a monastic retreat; but he had belied his early promise and become a powerful and ruthless warrior, renouncing his early vows and religious chants for the panegyrics of his court minstrels. We are still in the Heroic Age of Wales, and all that Gildas tells us of the splendid and imposing figure of Maelgwn and his career is typical of a heroic prince; but this is also the Age of the Saints, and it is characteristic of the period that warrior princes in all the Celtic countries of Britain may leave the world to enter monastic retreats, and often emerge again, whether temporarily or permanently, to take up arms as warrior kings.

Both Maelgwn and his son Rhyn are known to us chiefly through the wealth of traditions which became attached to them in later times, such as the medieval story of *Taliesin*, and the *Dream of Rhonabwy*, and the brief narratives incorporated in the Welsh Laws. Two generations later we enter a different world with King Cadfan, whose famous inscription with its inscribed cross in the Church of Llangadwaladr, speaks to us directly. The family seat at Aberffraw is a stone's throw away over a sandy flat which must have been ideal for the exercise of their members' horses. The inscription reads: *Catamanus rex, sapientisimus, opinatisimus omnium regum*, 'King Cadfan, most cultured and renowned of all kings.' Both inscription and lettering are in the most up-to-date form of Continental script,

Plate 16

Plate 18

and the little court of Aberffraw on the west coast of Anglesey [9]
was probably in direct touch with Continental culture. The
inscription suggests that Cadfan himself was an educated man
—*sapiens* means an educated man, and therefore a cleric at this
period; and the ambitious and high-toned epitaph with its
inscribed cross was doubtless set up by his son Cadwallon or
his grandson Cadwaladr, the traditional founder of the church
in which the inscription stands, the Westminster Abbey of the
family.

From first to last this was a brilliant dynasty. Cadfan's son,
the great Cadwallon, ally of Penda of Mercia, was the most
powerful enemy of the English in the north. He was killed
in battle near Hexham in 633 after his defeat by the Northumbrian king Oswald. The kingdom of Northumbria may well
owe its survival to the deaths of Urien or Rheged and Cadwallon, killed within a few years of one another after carrying
victory into the very heart of enemy territory.

Plate 19

We now enter upon the most momentous phase of Welsh
history, leading to the control of North Wales by the line of
Rhodri *Mawr* ('the Great'), who was killed in 878, and under
whose grandson, Hywel *Dda* ('the Good') the union with
England took place. This was the period during which, in
the course of a few generations, the Welsh kingdoms became
largely united by a series of royal marriage alliances. Hardly
less important is the part played in Welsh politics by the royal
House of Wessex, especially by Alfred the Great. His influential relations with a pro-English party in South Wales
paved the way for the union with England, cemented only a
generation later by Hywel Dda and Athelstan. The importance
of Alfred's policy to the west of Offa's Dyke, and the part
played by his Celtic sympathies and influence, are a much
neglected element of much importance in the history of the
British struggle against the Vikings.

Early in the ninth century a break took place in the normal patrilinear succession in Gwynedd. The throne was occupied by a certain Merfyn Frych (d. 844), the father of Rhodri Mawr. He is generally regarded as a stranger, and as inheriting through his mother Ethyllt, who was in the direct line of descent from the 'Island Dragon', Maelgwn, and whose father and grandfather were important enough to be mentioned in the Irish annals. King Cadfan of the famous inscription was one of Merfyn's ancestors on his mother's side, and so also was the great Cadwallon, enemy and slayer of King Edwin of Northumbria. On his mother's side Merfyn's credentials could not be better. But what do we know about the origins of his father?

Poetry and genealogies alike point to the Men of the North—both the great Dumbarton dynasty, and the families descended from Coel Hen, who had policed our northern frontiers for centuries at the close of the Roman period, and more recently had distinguished themselves in warfare against the powerful kingdom of Antrim in Ireland. The annals of this period, both Irish and Northumbrian, suggest that the westward thrust and expansion of Northumbria was causing a movement of the Britons of Strathclyde and Cumbria across the Narrow Seas from Galloway to seek territory in Ireland and the Isle of Man, and among them the paternal ancestors of Merfyn of Gwynedd. Again, the names Elidyr and Gwriad, not common elsewhere in Wales, but prominent in Merfyn's family, also point to an ultimate origin in the North, probably through Manx intermediaries. Further, the Irish Annals record the death in 657 of *Guret* (*Gwriad*), king of Dumbarton, while the famous Manx cross, inscribed *Crux Guriat*, of ninth-century date (cf. p. 121 below), suggests Merfyn's more immediate origin. Finally, we may point to references to the family in Welsh bardic poetry, and in a Triad to 'Merfyn Frych from the land of Manau'.

Merfyn's court in Gwynedd was a centre of some culture, and a meeting-place for Irish scholars en route from Ireland to western courts on the Continent. The earliest Welsh letter extant contains a greeting from '*Mermin* (Merfyn) *rex*' to a certain Concenn, probably Cyngen the last king of Powys, who died on a pilgrimage to Rome in 855, and whose sister, Nest, Merfyn married. The letter was eventually forwarded to an Irish teacher Colgu, and refers to certain Irish scholars, pupils of Colgu, who were at the time sojourning at the '*arx* (citadel) of *Mermin gloriosus*', apparently on their way to the Continent, and it has been happily preserved for us by a Continental scholar Dufthach into whose hand it had come.[10] Like Cadfan's inscription a century earlier, it sheds an interesting sidelight on the Continental communications and external culture of the west Welsh seaboard.

The marriage of Merfyn to Nest,[11] the sister of Cyngen, king of Powys, was one of the diplomatic marriages between the royal houses of the Welsh kingdoms. On Merfyn's death in 844 he was succeeded by his son Rhodri Mawr, and on Cyngen's death in 855 Rhodri seems to have inherited Powys through his mother. He ruled till 878, but his reign was a continuous struggle against external aggression from Mercia in the east, and the Danes in the west. This is the period to which Sir Ifor Williams[12] assigns the composition of the tragic poems which claim to be by a seventh-century Welsh poet Llywarch Hen, lamenting an English raid on Pengwern (Shrewsbury) that had left it a smoking ruin, and its princes slain (cf. pp. 106 f. below).

By a marriage with the sister of the king of Cardigan, Rhodri acquired the whole of south-west Wales except Dyfed, which was thus isolated. The dynasty of Gwynedd was a remarkable one. Within three generations, by a series of diplomatic marriages with Welsh princesses of the original ruling lines of the small kingdoms, they had made themselves masters of more than half Wales, apparently without striking a blow. The greater part of Wales had passed from a series of small independent kingdoms to something approaching a centralised monarchy, and Rhodri was now the greatest power in Wales. Henceforth the real struggle in the power politics of Wales was between Rhodri and North Wales on the one hand, and Alfred the Great and Wessex in close alliance with South Wales on the other. The two greatest personalities in Britain faced one another across Offa's Dyke.

Meanwhile, like Alfred himself, Rhodri concentrated all his best energies to retain Wales intact against the Danes. Anglesey had been devastated in 854 by the 'Black Gentiles', and though the Irish annals record the death of their leader, Gorm, by 'Ruaidhri [i.e. Rhodri], son of Mermin [i.e. Merfyn], king of the Britons' in 877, Rhodri himself had been forced to flee to Ireland after another severe attack by the 'Black Gentiles' on Anglesey. He had, in fact, a double front to defend; and the next year evidently found him back in Wales, for the *Annales Cambriae* record the death of both Rhodri and his son Gwriad at the hand of the Saxons. This was the consummation of the struggle for power between Gwynedd and Wessex. No *Life* of Rhodri has come down to us, but he is mentioned three times in the *Annals of Ulster*, and his court at Gwynedd, like that of his father Merfyn, was apparently still in touch with the Continent, for two poems by Sedulius Scotus, one a panegyric on a certain *Roricus* (this name is a Latinisation of *Rhodri*), and another a *carmen* celebrating a victory over the Norsemen, have been thought to have reference to Rhodri Mawr.[13] Charles the Bald, king of the Western Franks, was suffering heavily at the hands of the Danes at this time, and it would be natural for his court poets to extol the Welsh king who had slain their most formidable leader, and whose name, like that of his father, was in all probability already familiar to the Frankish court.

On Rhodri's death his realm was divided among his sons, and Asser tells us in his *Life of Alfred the Great* (ch. 80) that they terrorised the rest of the South Welsh kings, who appealed, one by one, in panic to Alfred for protection. The passage is full of interest, giving us an inventory of the reigning South Welsh kings of Alfred's day. The kingdoms had apparently changed little since their establishment at the close of the Roman period. Moreover, Alfred himself, no less than Rhodri, had built up a solid realm out of what had been virtually in-dependent units. It is interesting to speculate to what extent the death of Rhodri, by removing the fear of an attack from Gwynedd, contributed to lighten Alfred's task. From now on his most serious danger was from the east, and he was free to concentrate on the military measures against his eastern enemies to which the *Anglo-Saxon Chronicle* ascribes his whole success.

Nevertheless Alfred was evidently well aware that his military efforts against the Danes would have had little chance of success if he had been attacked simultaneously by enemies in his rear, whether from Wales or Ireland, and his relations with both were evidently close. Asser tells us that he contributed annually a part of his income to the Irish Church, and the Parker Text of the *Anglo-Saxon Chronicle* (annal 891) relates the arrival of three Irish pilgrims at his court, naming them by name, and adding incidentally a notice of the death of a famous Irish scholar. With Wales Alfred's relations were closer, and by a master-stroke of diplomacy he persuaded Asser, the Welsh scholar of St David's, to spend his time alternately at Alfred's court and at his own home in Dyfed, the most Irish, and therefore the most vulnerable part of Wales. In this way Asser was able to keep Alfred fully informed on South Welsh politics.

From a rousing contemporary patriotic Welsh poem, the *Armes Prydein* (cf. pp. 65 f. above), it is clear that Wales was now sharply divided between a strong anti-English party, chiefly in the north, led by the sons of Rhodri, and a South Welsh party which favoured union with England. Their leader in the first part of the tenth century was Hywel Dda, grandson of Rhodri,[14] who had added south-west Wales to his domain and ensured the friendship of the ruler of Dyfed by marrying his daughter. From 942 onwards he seems to have been almost the sole ruler of Wales under the English king Athelstan, with whom he associated himself closely, witnessing Athelstan's grants of lands and charters.[15] The British Museum possesses a charter, believed to be an original document, recording a grant of land by Athelstan at Luton in 931, which bears the testimony:

Ego Howael subregulus consensi et subscripsi.

Plate 20

The Museum also possesses what is believed to be the first pre-Conquest silver penny current under a Welsh king. On the obverse it bears the legend *Howael rex*, and on the reverse the name of the moneyer *Gillys*. It is thought that probably our silver penny was struck at Chester during the last years of Hywel's reign.[16] It should be added that Hywel's epithet *Dda* ('the Good') is given to no other Welsh king, and it was probably first given to him by the party in South Wales which favoured the union with Athelstan; the epithet *Mawr* ('Great'), applied to Rhodri, probably arose as an expression of the traditional North Welsh more exclusive nationalist policy.

Institutions, Architecture and Way of Life

THE INSTITUTIONS of the Celtic countries of Britain vary considerably because of the very wide differences in their origins and early political history. The Irish, the Welsh (including the Britons of southern Scotland) and the Dálriadic Scots, are all primarily a pastoral cattle-keeping people, with many ancient customs and institutions in common. Nevertheless the Picts, the Irish of Dálriada, and the Britons between the two walls each developed individually. Wales on the other hand is a much more self-contained and homogeneous country; but the English influence had to some extent penetrated into the customs of the South Welsh court before the codification of the Welsh laws. Welsh written law represents the modified laws and customs of Wales.

Apart from the stone inscriptions, funerary in character, and recording little more than proper names, the earliest information which we possess of individuals in Britain after the Roman Occupation is derived from their oral poetry. Although this was not written down before the ninth century, and is preserved in manuscripts of a still later date, a considerable body is believed to have been transmitted faithfully by the bards from the sixth and seventh centuries. We can accept their pictures of the time as virtually a contemporary record. The function of the bards was to record and to extol the life of their patrons, a society which had no other form of day-to-day journalism and propaganda. It follows that the records of the bards will be true within certain well-defined limits; but only partially true, and not an exact reflection of the society to which they belong (cf. p. 79 below).

Our chief body of early bardic poetry, and consequently our most intimate knowledge of early Celtic society in Britain, is that of the Britons of southern Scotland. At the close of the Roman period the Celtic peoples of the north, like the Britons of the south, had developed a society largely dependent on personal initiative, involving strength of character and individuality. The heroic ideals actuating these leaders of a society struggling for survival have inspired every poem which has come down to us, and at the same time they interpret for us the inevitable failure of such a society to survive in the modern world.

This early British society constituted what we have come to call a Heroic Age, and has been described in ch. III above. Their cohesion was fluid, depending on the personal loyalty of a *teulu* ('war-band') or *comitatus* ('personal military bodyguard') to their leaders, to whom they looked for support in time of peace, and towards whom in time of war they recognised and fulfilled their obligations. The leaders themselves obtained their prestige by right of their ancient hereditary aristocratic lineage, and depended on their own prowess and reputation to maintain it. To extol and enhance this prestige of the military leaders was the chief function of the bards. Such a society knows nothing of an ordered state, and lacks the first principle of survival, the ability to combine and subordinate the individual to a centralised and stabilised order.

Accordingly the Britons of southern Scotland, having no organised state, had no developed trade or coinage, no architecture except in wood and earth and rough stone forts. It is to be suspected that the chiefs tended to occupy Roman centres, both here and in Wales and elsewhere. The British prince Gwenddoleu, who was killed at the battle of Arthuret, had his seat at Caerwhinley, a name which may well be derived from Caer Gwenddoleu (cf. p. 64 above), and which was probably situated in the Roman fort at Netherby, near Longtown in the north of Cumberland. A similar overlap is perhaps to be found at Carlisle, almost certainly Urien's centre, on the great Roman road to the north.

The society presented to us by the bards is that of a military aristocracy with its inevitable emphasis on *noblesse oblige,* and on heroic honour. The qualities most prized in chiefs of these little local British courts were courage and generosity; in those of their followers, loyalty and gratitude, and services rendered, in return for past support and benefits received. A prince and his followers lived in close proximity to one another, sharing the evening feast and its accompaniment of music and song. In time of war they moved as one man, following their chief unquestioningly to victory or to death. The heroic poets give us a picture of life as they saw it in their professional capacity in small courts and small communities, where their songs could be heard by all and were well paid for. Personal and specific details are the essence of heroic poetry and the source of the minstrel's livelihood. His audience, the *teulu,* did not understand policy or organisation, and a minstrel who sang of such things would quickly starve. His is therefore a somewhat distorted picture of an irresponsible adolescent society, unproductive and largely predatory; occupied in warfare and hunting, fond of display and of horses, fine clothes, fine showy weapons; a society proud, boastful and honourable. Yet these intrepid northern heroes of the ancient Celtic world were Christians, and though the records of their Church have perished, later traditions would suggest that they shared the ideals and standards of the rest of the early Celtic Church.

Our earliest picture, then, of the Britons of the sixth and seventh centuries, is largely based on poetical records of the Britons of southern Scotland, supported as it is by the slender notes of Nennius; and we may safely take it as true of a wider area also. Gildas's picture of Maelgwn Gwynedd, the great North Welsh prince of his own day, is just such a Heroic Age prince, a Christian sojourning in youth in a monastic retreat, developing in later life into a ruthless warrior, and exchanging the monastic psalms for the panegyrics chanted to him by his minstrels at the feast. We have, however, to bear in mind that policy and some measure of constructive planning on the part of the leaders is necessary to enable even a Heroic Society to hold together and survive for a time.

We have some knowledge of a traditional framework of government for each of the Celtic countries; and from their legal documents we can reconstruct a widespread system of economic and hereditary law for both Wales and southern Scotland, and these can be supplemented from the far greater and better preserved body of Irish law. In general such laws, common to all the Celtic peoples of our Islands, represent the traditional customs of a community whose wealth is largely in cattle. Fines are computed in cows and in slaves. But the British have relatively little to tell us of the legal status of women and their property rights, such as we have in the Irish Laws,[1] and nothing of the elaborate provisions for sick maintenance and treatment, of which the Irish Laws give us elaborate information.[2]

We know, however, from references in the Welsh Laws[3] that, like the Irish, they represent codification of custom compiled and modified from time to time by professional lawyers before they were written down in the form in which they have been recorded under the name of King Hywel Dda in the tenth century (cf. p. 86 below). We can trace adaptation to changing conditions. Moreover, the Welsh Laws have an archaic stratum which can sometimes be detected with the help of the Irish legal texts. It is remarkable that nearly all their basic legal terms are native—such terms as court, judge, claim, prosecution, penalty, contract, surety, debtor, creditor, and others. This, as Binchy points out, suggests that the Romanisation of the British tribes must have been very superficial.[4]

The most important of the Celtic institutions is the kingship, which is universal, though there are some important differences as between individual Celtic countries. In Wales the old Celtic word for king (*rí*) went out of use early, its place and functions being taken by rulers known under various names such as *arglwyd* ('lord'), *tywysog* ('prince'), *brenhin* ('king'), the three terms being legally synonymous. The old word survives, however, in the feminine *rhiain,* used of a 'dame' or 'lady', and appears in the literary name *Rhiannon*, the queen of the super-natural regions. In historical times we know of no ruling queen among the Welsh or the Irish of Argyll, but in Wales there are an appreciable number of instances of succession through the female. Each *brenhin* had a court or *llys*, his royal seat, some-times fortified; and here also he literally held court and tried suits, local custom dictating the verdict of a jury in such suits.

The exact meaning of Pictish kingship is not clear, nor is the relationship of the various provinces in the early period. In one of the medieval surveys of Pictavia we read of *regna*, and the Irish annals speak of a 'king of Fortrenn', but we cannot be sure that these terms are used strictly. Bede speaks (*H.E.* V, 21) of a *rex Pictorum,* but he refers to the Picts in general under various terms—*gens, provincia, natio.* Adamnán (II, 42) refers to a *regulus* ('petty king') of the Orkneys.

It is in regard to the succession to the kingship that the Celtic countries differed most from one another. In Wales succession was patrilinear, but not necessarily following primo-geniture. In all the Celtic countries tribal kingship was in theory open to every adult male member of the royal line whose great-grandfather or nearer ascendant had been king. As official heir to the throne he had special legal privileges, and in Wales was termed *gwrthrychiad* (lit. 'one who looks forward', or 'expects'). Asser of Wales uses the word *secundarius* for the appointed heir, and the term in use in the Welsh laws is *edling*, which has been borrowed from the Anglo-Saxon *aetheling.* In the laws of Hywel Dda the right to nominate his successor is assigned to the king. The successor here may be his son or his brother or his paternal nephew, whereas under the old system a much larger number of relatives were eligible. The Codes suggest that succession was settled during the lifetime of the reigning king or chief, but in the historical period the genealogies suggest that for both the Welsh and the North British patrilineal succession from father to son was almost universal. In Dálriada, however, the custom prevailed which is known as *tanistry* (*tánaise rí*, second to a king), which is patrilineal, but by which kings were succeeded, not by their sons directly, but by their brothers in the first instance, and then by their nephews. The practice of direct patrilineal succession does occur in Dálriada in the time of Aidán mac Gabráin where Adamnán relates (I, 9) that Aidán appointed one of his sons to succeed him as a matter of course; but this is perhaps one of the Welsh elements which we know to have been introduced into the royal House of Argyll at this time (cf. p. 48 above). The custom of tanistry was, however, general till a late period.

The Pictish law of succession differed fundamentally from those of the other British kingdoms. This is indeed the most remarkable of their institutions. Bede was aware of succession through the female as a living custom among the Picts in his day. He writes (*H.E.* II, i): 'Whenever doubt arises they will choose their king by the female rather than the male ancestry of their kings,' and he adds that 'everyone knows that this custom is still maintained among the Picts.'

Antiquarian tracts bear out Bede's statement in general, and in the third Pictish king-list (cf. p. 58 above) only two kings have names attached to them of fathers who have reigned. There is no clear evidence of succession through the fathers' line till the ninth century, but a record of the fathers of the reigning kings is believed to have been kept, perhaps from the fifth century. Kings married and had families and homes more or less permanent, but their sons could not succeed. The fathers of the kings are sometimes foreigners,[5] and this may in fact have been usual. The organisation of the royal family seems to have been in general matrilocal as well as matrilineal, but not in general matriarchal.[6]

Among all the Celtic peoples the tie of kindred was the strongest and most enduring of all their early institutions.

In pre-Norman Wales the people as a whole were divided into two principal classes:

(1) the so-called free tribesmen, known by various names, the *uchelwyr, breyr,* and *innate boneddig,* who were the dominant class, presumably descended from the conquering Cymric (Celtic) population; and

(2) the unfree, or subject populations, known variously as *taeog, aillt, alltud.*

The free tribesmen are exclusively those who claim blood relationship, and are the members of the *cenedl* ('kindred group'). The unfree class of whatever origin were not included among the tribesmen, and were not subject to the rights and responsibilities of the *cenedl.* In general they carried on the agricultural work of the community. Below these were the class of slaves, the actual property of their owners, to whom a large part of the manual labour fell.[7]

The *cenedl* formed the basis of society, the kindred or clan, the family in the wide sense of the Scottish clans today, claiming to be descended from a common ancestor, within the ninth degree, through the male line within various strictly recognised grades of relationship. As Giraldus Cambrensis observes, 'The most ordinary folk among this people keep careful count of the family pedigree.' [8] At the head of each unit of the *cenedl* was a single 'head'—a *pencenedl.*[9] Perhaps the most interesting feature of the *cenedl* is that it functioned for legal purposes much as the individual does in modern society. The *cenedl* 'hung together', a wrong done to one of its members was a wrong to the 'kindred' as a whole, to be avenged by them as a whole, the responsibility of each member being apportioned according to his status within the 'nine degrees' of the *cenedl*. A crime perpetrated by one member must be expiated by the *cenedl* as a whole, according to a similar scale of responsibility.

Perhaps the most telling illustration, both of the solidarity and of the practical working of the *cenedl* in legal proceedings, is the vendetta or 'blood-feud', which was still active in early Wales; but by the time of the formulation of the early laws into a system it had become a recognised custom for the kindred of the slain man to accept compensation by the payment of *galanas,* 'blood money' or *wergild,* the amount being fixed according to the rank of the slain. 'They are ready', says Giraldus again, 'to avenge not only new and recent injuries, but also ancient and bygone ones, as though but recently received.' Similarly, in the compensation (*sarhad*) due for the lesser crime of insult or injury short of homicide, the *cenedl* as far as the second cousin had joint responsibility for the crimes of their kinsmen,[10] the Welsh law codes, like the Anglo-Saxon, containing precise regulations for payment of every limb and member of the body injured.

The operation of *galanas* and *sarhad,* like many other of the Welsh laws and customs, was evidently equally operative in southern Scotland. No codes have survived, but the perpetuation of these ancient institutions is proved by the continuous enactments to abolish what remained of them, more especially of those of the Britons and the Scots. The laws of King David of Scotland show distinct traces of the *wergild* and the responsibility of the *cenedl* for its payment, mostly in cows;[11] in the twelfth century the 'law which is called *weregylt*' is still specified and assessed in cattle, and the continued right of vengeance on the part of the kindred of the slain is still recognised. The social classes continue to be referred to under certain

Celtic titles, e.g. in the treatise *Regiam Majestatem*, where the Scottish compiler has added to his work a quite independent document of much earlier date.[12] A particularly interesting late code of North British Laws is known as the *Leges inter Brettos et Scottos*,[13] where the compiler must have made use of some older system of laws in the language of Cumbria, for three technical legal terms have been preserved in Cumbric, all having close relations in the legal terminology of early Wales. The regulations consist of fines for certain offences referred to under their Welsh terms, and all assessed in cows. The laws have probably been formulated in the early part of the eleventh century when the king was seeking to regulate relations between the very diverse elements of the united Scotland.[14]

In Wales the chief units of administration are the *tref*, the *cantref*, and the *commote*. The *tref* is the smallest unit and originally meant a 'house' or dwelling-place. The free landowners lived, not in villages, but at some distance from one another, as is natural in pastoral communities; and the free *tref* formed the unit associated in the family property, whether for payment of dues for the upkeep of the court, or for the inheritance of land among the *cenedl*. In addition to the free *tref* there existed also a *taeogtref*, or village community of unfree, i.e. servile, tenants, who shared joint responsibility for the tilling of the soil and had certain privileges (such as ploughing rights) in common, and this unit seems to have corresponded approximately to the Anglo-Saxon *tun*. A still smaller unit of the *taeogtref*, was the *tyddyn*, a tiny hamlet comprising a farm and the cottages of the farm-'hands', the *tyddyn* being frequently four in number to a *taeogtref*, and sharing a church in common.

According to tradition the whole country was divided into *cymwyds* (Angl. '*commotes*'), corresponding to the division employed in the Welsh Laws (cf. p. 80 above), and possibly relatively late. The *commote* comprised a large number of *trefs*, grouped together for purposes of administration.[15] The *commotes* were grouped in small units of two, three, or four, to form a still larger division known as a *cantref* (*lit.* 'a hundred *trefs*'), and were in fact the basic unit into which, at least in late times, the whole country was divided. 'Thus,' as Edwards says, 'the commote was the basic subdivision in a hierarchy of subdivisions, and was as definite an institution in medieval Wales as was the hundred in England.'[16]

In the laws it is the *commote* which appears to be the living and active body, the references to the *cantref* being for the most part literary, with a smack of antiquity about them.[17] In the medieval traditional stories of Wales known as the *Mabinogion* (cf. p. 110 below), the *cantref* is the territorial division of Wales invariably referred to; and still in everyday speech today Cardigan Bay is commonly referred to as the *Cantref y Gwaelod,* recalling the mythical kingdom ruled by Seithenyn, which became inundated by the sea, and disappeared for ever under what is now Cardigan Bay. It will be seen that modifications have taken place from the earliest times to the period when a written code was formulated. The legal code represents an organism rather than a creation or enactment.

The Welsh code of laws is our most important and earliest surviving monument of the institutions of Celtic Britain.[18] All versions of its preamble claim that it was promulgated by the South Welsh king, Hywel Dda (cf. p. 80 above) from his seat known as *Ty Gwyn,* 'The White House', on the River Taf, and allusions throughout the text also refer to the code of Hywel. The preambles are without doubt all later. The Preamble claims that Hywel assembled representatives from throughout his kingdom to codify and unify variant local and tribal practices. There were in Wales trained laymen and judges whose duty it was to ensure the faithful transmission and execution of earlier codes, and various such authorities are cited in the code itself. Evidently there were also written law books earlier than that of Hywel, but they have not survived. The earliest extant manuscript is written in Latin and that was probably its original language; all our manuscripts are later than 1150, and represent editions compiled from time to time by later district lawyers. Three of these later recensions differing considerably from one another are extant, and many glosses and much illustrative matter have crept into the text.

The 'Laws' are a strange document. They tell us perhaps more about the court and its officials in Hywel's day than of earlier times, and there is no doubt that the picture of the court here presented has been influenced from England. Nevertheless it throws much light on early Wales. The court was made up of twenty-four officers, and their duties, rights, and perquisites occupy most of the first part of the code and throw light on many matters of court life, such as the social status of military and civil officials and the emoluments of the members of the royal households. Regulations relating to court officials include their duties and their privileges and remuneration, their daily routine, and even the clothes they wore. Among the most interesting are the sections relating to the *penkerd,* 'the chief of song', and the *bard teulu,* 'the bard of the royal entourage'. The former has his land free, and sits next to the *edling* (cf. p. 81 above) in the hall, and his function is to sing to the king. The *bard teulu* also has his land free and his horse from the king, as well as his harp and a gold ring from the queen; but he sings only after the *penkerd,* and his seat in the hall is lower, and when the queen wishes to hear a song in her bower he must sing to her three songs softly lest the hall be disturbed.

An important, and doubtless more ancient, section of the laws consists of a penal code, regulating the penalties for murder and theft and for *galanas* and *sarhad* (cf. p. 84 above); and the law of inheritance is clearly provided for.

A third section regulates valuations and fines. An interesting part fixes values of property, such as the king's barn, a sword

Fig. 12. Detail of the monogram beginning St Mark's Gospel in the Book of Kells (Irish)

with a gold hilt, a harp and its tuning key—both separately assessed—as being essential to the minstrel's livelihood. Valuations of livestock are laid down, e.g. bees, which we are gravely assured have their origin in Paradise. The most entrancing of these intimate glimpses of life in early Wales is the penalty for killing or stealing a cat which guards the king's barn—'Its head is to be held downwards on a clean, level floor, and its tail is to be held upwards; and after that wheat must be poured over it until the tip of its tail is hidden, and that is its value.'

To which a further gloss adds a note on the *teithi* ('points') of a well-bred cat: 'It should be perfect of ear, perfect of eye, perfect of teeth, perfect of claw, without marks of fire, and it should kill mice, and not devour its kittens, and should not go caterwauling every new moon.'

Plate 21

Readers of the Medieval English text of the 'Rule for Ankeresses' will appreciate the value of the cat in medieval times to guard stores, and its importance is fully recognised by the sculptor of the Monasterboice high cross in Ireland, and by the illuminator of the Book of Kells; but the Welsh are the only *Fig. 12* people who have introduced the cat into their laws in a spirit of light humour.

Nothing in the Laws of Hywel Dda, or indeed in any laws of the Celtic people, suggests the existence of town life or of organised commerce, and the total absence of native coinage or any system of weights and measures would seem to preclude extensive trade, though barter must have been practised extensively, even with foreign countries. The contemporary *Life of St John the Almsgiver,* Patriarch of Alexandria, written by his countryman, Leontius of Cyprus, some time after 641, relates (ch. 10) that while a famine was raging in Britain a ship laden with corn was sent there from Alexandria by the Patriarch; on arrival it traded its freight of corn, receiving half a 'nomisma' for each bushel, in addition to half a full ship's freight of tin.[19]

Evidence of trade between the west of Britain and the East Mediterranean world from the fifth to the seventh century is increasing. A tiny fortified enclosure, less than a third of an acre in extent, at Dinas Powis in Glamorgan yielded sherds of Mediterranean pottery and amphorae, and glass beakers probably from Merovingian Gaul, testify to foreign trade; the massive fortifications suggest the stronghold of an affluent Welsh chieftain and his immediate family on what is apparently an Iron Age site.[20] A trading station, probably of the fifth or sixth century, located at Bantham in south Devon,[21] has produced pottery of East Mediterranean type, and similar pottery has been found at Tintagel on the north Cornish coast,[22] at Gwithian in west Cornwall, and even as far north as Dunadd; which suggests that pottery and other commodities were being brought by sea from the Byzantine world in the sixth century.

In general, the material culture and economic well-being of

Fig. 13

Fig. 14

Fig. 13. Slab with Pictish incised bull, Burghead, Elgin (after Allen and Anderson)

the Celtic peoples of our period were not far advanced. All counted their chief wealth in cattle. In Wales their seasonal nomadism is enshrined in their place-names, such as the very common *hafod*, and *hafoty*, the 'summer hill pasture' and 'summer dairy' and its *ty*, 'dwelling', 'cot'. Their forays and cattle raids were small-scale depredations made among neighbours, natural enough where food organisation had not developed. Agriculture was carried on, as the wheat impressions in some of the hand-made local pottery show; but it was on a relatively small scale. Their whole wealth in the ninth century is crudely summarised in the tribute exacted by the Saxon king Athelstan at Hereford—a tribute of gold, silver,

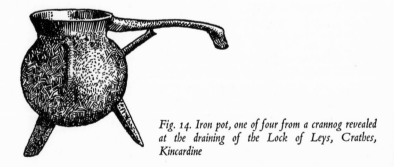

Fig. 14. Iron pot, one of four from a crannog revealed at the draining of the Lock of Leys, Crathes, Kincardine

cattle, hunting-dogs and hawks. It is the life of an aristocracy of
the open air; a life, in peace-time, of hunting, fishing and
cattle-keeping. Such a life inspired the little cradle song which
has somehow found its way into the text of the *Gododdin* (cf.
p. 104 below), sung by a nurse to the child Dinogat:

> When thy father went a-hunting   *Fig. 15*
> With spear on shoulder, and cudgel in hand,
> He would call his big dogs,
> 'Giff, Gaff': 'Catch, catch!' 'Fetch, fetch!'
> In his coracle he would spear a fish,
> Striking suddenly like a lion.
> When thy father went up the mountain
> He would bring back a roebuck, a wild boar, a stag,
> A spotted grouse from the mountain,
> A fish from the falls of Derwennydd.
> As many as thy father caught with his spear
> None would escape except those with wings.[23]

Our knowledge of the architectural monuments of the Celtic
peoples is confined largely at present to their fortifications and
hill-top citadels, but at Dinorben in Denbighshire traces of a
large circular house and an oblong aisled hall suggest ambitious
sub-Roman buildings probably of fourth-century date, on a
site going back to the Early Iron Age.[24] Earlier sites, both of the
Iron Age and of the Roman period, were frequently re-
occupied. The deserted Roman fort of Caer Gybi on Holyhead
was re-occupied, and a post-Roman addition made to *Y Gaer*
('the Fort') at Brecon. Castle Dore, 'King Mark's Castle', in
Cornwall, and Lydney Temple (cf. pp. 29, 36 above), both
have an Iron Age nucleus. The Iron Age sites of Garn   Plates 22, 23
Boduan and Tre'r Ceiri near Nevin in Caernarvonshire were
both reoccupied from the fifth to the seventh century.[25] Dinas
Emrys near Beddgelert in the same country shows an inter-
mittent or continuous occupation from the Early Iron Age, and

includes a small defensive fifth-century fort. Of great interest here is the evidence of foreign trade, including fragments of two classes of pottery similar to those found on Dark Ages sites in Cornwall, believed to be of Mediterranean origin, the most remarkable being a base of a pot stamped with the Christian symbols. Occupation of the homestead therefore clearly continued into the fifth century, and the second phase, with its fortifications, marks the conversion of the site into a Dark Age chieftain's stronghold.[26]

In recent years progress has been made towards a more scientific study of the different types of fortification.[27] In Scotland, important types are:

(1) oval or oblong forts with heavy stone walls; apparently chiefly within the main Pictish area;

(2) simple circular structures known as 'ring forts', widespread throughout the area of the Southern Picts, sometimes with auxiliary defensive works around them, or on the remains of earlier Iron Age forts, such as Turin Hill in Angus;

(3) citadel forts, in which the citadel is surrounded by contemporary earthworks, and generally placed on a rocky hilltop; such is Dumyat (Dunmyat) in the Ochils, probably, as its name suggests, a strong fortress of the Miathi (cf. p. 48 above). The most interesting of the earlier defensive structures of Scotland are the tower-like brochs; but these are essentially of the Iron Age or Roman periods, and only known to have been occasionally used later. Some important forts are referred to in historical records. Dunadd (cf. p. 60 above) was occupied intermittently from the early sixth till the ninth century.[28] Simpler structures are the duns of southern Scotland, consisting of a strong stone wall surrounding a flat, steep, even precipitous hill-top. In Wales, fortified enclosures designed to protect single families or very small communities are also coming to light, such as Castell Odo, near Aberdaron in Caernarvonshire,[29] and Dinas Powis (cf. p. 89 above).

Plates 24, 25

An interesting form of architecture is the long, shallow, underground 'earth-house', or 'souterrain',[30] found throughout the early British area, and heavily concentrated in Scotland in the territory occupied by the Southern Picts, where they are popularly known as 'Pictish dwellings' or 'caves', or 'weems' (cf. Irish *uaimh*, 'a cave'). They are common also in Cornwall, where they are known as *fogous*[31]. The Fifeshire place-name *Wemyss* is doubtless derived from its concentration of natural coastal caves, but 'weems' are also found in Ireland, sometimes in pre-historic forts; one has even been discovered in the burial ground of the Protestant cathedral of Killala in Co. Mayo, and another in the churchyard of Glen Colum-cille in Co. Donegal. Their purpose is unknown, but some are evidently post-Roman in date, or perhaps in reconstruction, for Roman worked stones have been built into the walls. In some instances traces of dwellings have been found on the surface above them. Perhaps they were originally larders, like our modern cellars. They are wholly unsuited for human habitation, even as places of refuge.

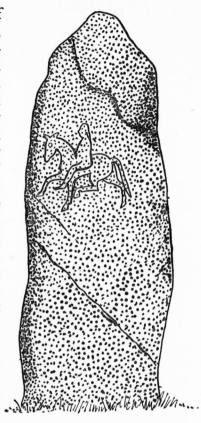

Fig. 15. Horseman. Pictish incised carved stone, Migvie, Aberdeenshire (after *Diack*). *Note the absence of stirrups*

Fig. 16

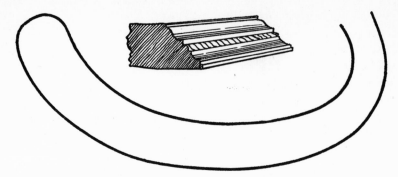

Fig. 16. Ground plan of earth house at Newstead, and stone with Roman moulding found in it, evidently part of a Roman cornice (after *Anderson*)

On the whole the majority of Celtic and Pictish dwellings will have been constructed of wood. The extensive use of iron in the period immediately preceding, resulting in the wide-spread felling of timber and the clearing of the land for more intensive agriculture, would doubtless make the felling of building timber an easier matter than stone quarrying. At the Roman camp at Inchtuthill in Perthshire the great amount of timber used produced for the excavators nearly 12 tons of iron nails.[32] That the British were not wholly ignorant of the amenities of civilised life is illustrated by an inscription at the monastic site of Maughold on the Isle of Man to a certain Branhui, who 'led off water to this place';[33] and in Wales the

Plate 26

Fig. 17

Romano-British village of Din Lligwy on Anglesey, believed to be a concentration of native British houses constructed in a Roman tradition, with formal rooms and stepped entrances, shows an appreciation of dignity in building. The upper classes were not so poor in material wealth and culture as the native manufactures would lead us to suppose.

Hoards discovered during the present century have produced treasures of considerable intrinsic and artistic value which show that, whether by trade, or exchange, or piracy, the Britons were

familiar with some of the best Continental objects of both
ceremonial and household use. The silver treasure of fourth-
century Continental origin discovered on Traprain Law in
Haddingtonshire in 1919 consisted largely of remains of a
superb table service, proving that such things were not outside
the possible possession of the British chieftains of southern Scotland in the fifth century. This hoard certainly contained loot,
for many of the objects had been ruthlessly cut in halves as if
for a crude 'sharing out' among raiders—'the veritable wealth of

Plates 27, 28

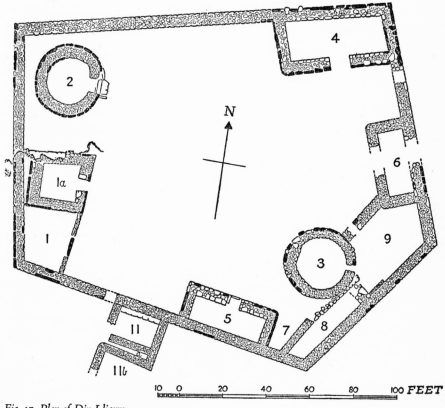

Fig. 17. Plan of Din Lligwy

95

Plate 29

Plates 30, 31

a robber band'.[34] The late Roman treasure reported in 1946 at Mildenhall in Suffolk,[35] like that of Traprain Law, is late Classical in origin and style, and again, like the latter, consists for the most part of fourth-century objects. These resemble the Balline Hoard[36] from Ireland, which was probably loot from Britain; but all show that silver objects of high quality were available in the Romano-British period. The Traprain Law treasure contained two silver spoons engraved with the Chi-Rho monogram, and the Mildenhall treasure had eight spoons, two of them christening spoons, as inscriptions within the bowl suggest, and their association with other plate shows that they were intended for use either in a church or in a wealthy Romano-British household.

In 1958 a superb treasure was brought to light by Professor O'Dell[37] on St Ninian's Isle in Shetland during the excavation of a little early Celtic church. The treasure had been roughly tumbled together into a box, and covered by a small slab lightly inscribed with a cross, and then buried hurriedly under the floor of the church. The circumstances of the burial are a complete mystery, for the objects are by no means all of ecclesiastical provenance, and though here too the treasure contained a spoon, it has no suggestion of ecclesiastical design. The hoard is indeed very 'mixed' in character. Some of the objects are in mint condition, others worn and even repaired, and their dates of origin cover a considerable period of time, probably between 700 and 800. The most likely explanation is a hurried burial of treasure a little before 800, perhaps due to panic in face of a Viking raid (see further pp. 139 f. below).

One of the most important Dark Age hoards found in a Celtic area of Britain comes from a spot remotely distant from Shetland. This is the silver treasure found in 1774 concealed in the débris of an old tin streamwork at Trewhiddle[38] on the south coast of Cornwall, and made up of various secular and ecclesiastical objects, not apparently all of the same date. The

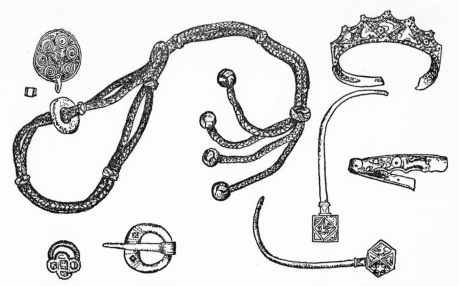

Fig. 18. The Trewhiddle hoard, St Austell, Cornwall (after Wilson, from Minute Book of the Soc. of Antiq.)

ecclesiastical objects include a unique example of a scourge of twisted silver wire, and a small silver chalice resembling that belonging to Hexham Abbey church and the famous Tassilo cup which can be dated to between 777 and 788. The form of ornamentation is comparable to that current in southern England at the end of the eighth century; and of over one hundred coins which have been recovered, the majority are of West Saxon and Mercian kings, and enable us to date the deposition of the treasure to 875. Both this date and the objects themselves suggest a Saxon rather than a Celtic background, although they were found in a British area; but they prove, like the other hoards, that the Celtic people of Britain were able to profit by the higher material culture of their neighbours.

Apart from a small hoard of coins found at Trewardreath, also in Cornwall, where they had been deposited about 928–930, the coins of the Trewhiddle hoard are the only Anglo-Saxon coins so far found in Cornwall. Indeed, early coin hoards of Anglo-Saxon origin are surprisingly rare in Celtic

Fig. 18

Plate 32

lands. The well-known hoard found in Bangor, Caernarvonshire,[39] is not earlier than the tenth century. The National Museum of Scotland possesses an Anglo-Saxon coin from Buston crannog, which shows contact with England.

Of the life of the poorer classes in our period we know little save by inference, but the excavation of *cytiau*, or native huts, by Mr Charles Philips at Pant y Saer in Anglesey[40] gives us our most illuminating picture of a native settlement of humble class. The homestead is believed to be a survival from the Roman period, lasting from the fourth to the sixth century, and consists of two circular stone huts within an oval walled enclosure, whose occupants grew grain on a terrace at a lower level, and kept cattle on higher ground hard by. The original internal arrangements at Pant y Saer were of the most primitive character. Later, two rectangular huts were added, from the largest

Plate 33

of which came a silver penannular brooch and some sherds of Roman pottery and crude native ware. The brooch is a rare example of sixth-century jewellery of good quality found in Wales, though bronze objects are not uncommon and include a penannular brooch, a ring-headed and a spiral-headed pin, all from South Wales; a few glass beads from Anglesey can also be dated to the sixth century.

Plate 32

Crannogs or pile dwellings were common in the Scottish lochs, and have been found also at Glastonbury and in Llangorse Lake in Brecknock. People lived in caves perhaps to a greater extent than is often realised. Scottish caves were occupied by hermits of the early Church and at least three caves in the Gower Peninsula in South Wales have yielded archaeological finds from between the Roman and the Norman periods, which include coins of Charlemagne, Lothair, and Ecgberht of Wessex, bronze annular brooches and other ornaments. Again, in the Lesser Garth cave in Glamorgan[41] miscellaneous objects of Irish type, and having parallels in Dunadd, suggest a date in the Early Christian period.[42]

Chapter VI

Literature

THE INTELLECTUAL LIFE of a people is most clearly seen in their literature. The art of writing in the Latin alphabet had been introduced into Britain in Roman times, when the country became nominally Christian. We have seen that alongside the Roman alphabet there had been in use, in both Ireland and Britain, probably from the fourth century, an alphabet peculiar to these lands and of native Celtic origin, known as *ogam*.[1] Both these alphabets have survived in Britain from the Roman period in stone inscriptions only. All our surviving examples, whether in the Latin alphabet, which are by far the most numerous, or in ogam, are brief funerary monuments. We have no examples of the use of the ogam alphabet for literary purposes.

Originally the literature of the Celtic peoples of Britain was oral, and there is a wide cultural and chronological gap between the original use of writing for brief inscriptions and perhaps other official purposes on the one hand, and its general use for what we commonly mean by literature on the other. Indeed the most important and the most interesting of the characteristics shared in common by all the Celtic peoples is the cultivation of oral literature. This art was ancient and was guarded and cultivated by a highly privileged class in every court. These repositories of the traditional oral literature had a long and honourable history, in direct descent from their ancestors in Gaul, where in early times they had been divided into several classes according to the specialised nature of their learning or their art.

Caesar speaks[2] of the professional class of the ancient Gauls as *druids*, to whom he ascribes judicial and priestly functions, and proficiency in natural philosophy and what relates to the gods. He reports them as responsible for the education of the young Gaulish nobility, and as carrying on this function during many years exclusively in oral poetry, though in almost all other matters they made use of the Greek alphabet in their public and private transactions. Caesar tells us further that the institution of the druids was believed to have originated in Britain, and that those who desired a fuller knowledge of the discipline still resorted to Britain to obtain it. Tacitus also tells us that the order flourished in Anglesey, and gives us a highly coloured picture of their reception of the Roman General Suetonius when he attacked the island.

In later times references to the druids in the British Isles are confined to Ireland, where they figure in the early sagas as possessed of supernatural powers, especially of prophecy, and where they hold a high position at the courts, in general one only residing in any court. A reference to the word *druí* occurs in the ancient Irish law-tracts of the eighth century or earlier, where the druid is seen shorn of his ancient high dignity, though still grudgingly granted a legal status.[3] Druids as such are not mentioned in connection with St Patrick before the *Tripartite Life* of the ninth century. Earlier sources speak of the saint's opponents simply as *magi*. Where British historical documents mention men of supernatural pretensions, such as Broichán, the *magus* of Brude mac Maelchon, referred to by Adamnán in his *Life* of Saint Columba, these are not to be interpreted as *druids*, who constitute a specific class. Broichán is also referred to by Adamnán as the *nutritor*[4] or 'fosterer' of Brude, and he also refers to Joseph as the *nutritor* of Jesus Christ; the word is also applied by Gildas (ch. 28) to the two 'guardians' of the princes of Dumnonia.

Strabo speaks of two other professional classes among the ancient Gauls, whom he calls *vates* and *bardoi*. The *vates*, like the druids, appear to have survived in ancient Ireland, under the term *filid* (sing. *fili*; lit. 'seers'), and to have combined the intellectual functions of both the druids and the *vates* of Gaul, being the professional class of oral traditional knowledge, which they transmitted in poetry. The ancient class of poets known in Gaul as *bardoi* were composers of panegyric songs, and are doubtless represented by the court bards of both Ireland and Wales. Indeed, in Britain the distinction between the early professional classes was no longer observed, and the term 'bard' is in general use in Welsh literature for all professional poets. It seems to have been usual in both Ireland and Britain for a single official bard to have been attached to each court, though we occasionally hear of bards visiting more than one court, and certain courts and princes acquired a reputation as special patrons of the bards. Taliesin addresses elegies to Urien of Rheged in the North, and to his son Owein, as well as to Cynan Garwyn in Powys in Wales, and to Gwallawg, ruler of the British kingdom of Elmet in Yorkshire. He seems to have sojourned at the courts of both Rheged and Powys, whether as a visiting bard, or as a more or less permanent court poet.

The court of Powys in eastern Wales was at all times a great centre of poetry, and here we find reference to Taliesin singing at the court of Cynan Garwyn, son of Brochfael Ysgythrog, who is probably the Brochfael present at the time of the attack by the Northumbrian king Aethelfrith at the Battle of Chester in 616. Indeed, one of the earliest bardic poems which has come down to us is believed to be the *Trawsganu Kynan Garwyn mab Brochfael*,[5] composed in an archaic form of Welsh, and among the small group of authentic contemporary poems of Taliesin addressed to this prince. In a later poem, Taliesin claims to have sung at the court of Powys to Cynan's father:

> I sang in the meadows of the Severn
> Before an illustrious lord,
> Before Brochfael of Powys
> Who loved my *awen* ('poetic inspiration').

The son of this Cynan Garwyn was the prince Selyf who lost his life in the battle of Chester (see above), and whose own court bard Arofan was remembered for many centuries thereafter as setting the standard of high perfection in his art.

In the early British courts, essentially heroic, individualistic and aristocratic, it is believed that the bard's most important function was that of custodian of the genealogies. In countries with no written laws, or charters, or wills, genealogies were the only guarantee of the right to a share in land, and of the right to inherit. The chiefs depended largely on the bards for their prestige and reputation. Where there were no newspapers or leading articles, all political and personal propaganda was in the hands of the court poets, and the closest personal tie existed between the poet and his patron. It is not surprising that traditions have come down to us of bards who have killed themselves on the death of their lord. We have seen, for example, that British poetical tradition represents the poet Myrddin as losing his wits after the death of his lord Gwenddoleu in the battle of Arthuret (cf. p. 64 above).

Almost all our early Welsh poetry is preserved in four medieval manuscripts dating from *c.* 1150–1350. Religious poetry is also preserved in three of these manuscripts; but the majority of the poems are in the native Welsh tradition, though Christian allusions are common, as is natural in the poetry of a Christian people. The metres are native Welsh metres, but Latin influence is ultimately responsible for the stanzaic form, and the use of rhyme. The poems show great variety, in both form and subject. The most striking feature is that in Welsh, as in the earliest Irish poetry, narrative is wholly absent. Most of the poems are composed in the form of panegyrics and elegies, and there is also a certain amount of occasional poetry, and poetry of celebration, whether of triumph or disaster. The *mise-en-scène,* the events which form the subjects, and the persons taking part are indicated by allusion and reference. It is assumed that the audience is familiar with the background. The poems are, in fact, contemporary in form with the events.

The poetry of this early period relates to the sixth and seventh centuries, and is known as the poetry of the *Cynfeirdd*, the 'early bards'. Among the most interesting is the *Eulogy of Cadwallon* (son of Cadfan, see p. 71 above), perhaps by his court bard Afan feddig (*B.B.C.S.* VII, 31). The majority are anonymous, but the names of four poets are recorded by Nennius in the *Historia Brittonum* (ch. 62). Immediately after his account of Ida and Outigern he has the following well-known passage:

> Then Talhaern Tataguen ('Father of inspiration') gained renown in poetry, and Neirin (less correctly but more usually called *Aneirin*) and Taliesin, and Bluchbard and Cian . . . gained renown together in British poetry.

An appreciable nucleus of the works attributed to Taliesin and Aneirin are believed to have been preserved. In the manuscript known as the *Book of Taliesin*, dating from *c.* 1275, Sir Ifor Williams has detected 'a hard core of twelve historical poems which deal with the sixth century'. Nine are in praise of Urien of Rheged and his son Owein; two in praise of Gwallawg (cf. p. 101 above) and one is addressed to Cynan Garwyn.

A unique manuscript, generally referred to as *The Book of Aneirin*, opens as follows:

> This is the Gododdin, Aneirin sang it.

It is a small book written *c.* 1250 in two hands; but of the one hundred and three stanzas which it contains about one fifth are copies from a ninth-century original. These were therefore in existence in written form about four centuries earlier than our manuscript, and so must in fact have been recorded at the same period as the earliest extant example of written Welsh poetry—the three stanzas in the so-called Juvencus MS., dating from the first half of the ninth century.

The *Gododdin* is the most famous of all the Cycles of early North British poetry.[6] It is a corpus of poems, largely elegiac in tone, most of which relate to a disastrous expedition against the Saxons undertaken *c.* 600 by the war-band of Mynyddawg Mwynvawr, a chief of Manau Gododdin, and which record the defeat of the Cymry in a great battle fought at a place called Catraeth, generally identified with Catterick Bridge in Yorkshire. No account of the battle as a whole appears anywhere, but we learn much incidentally from allusions in the poems —to the fine horses and equipment which the British troops had received from their leader, to the high promises they made to him in return as the expedition was planned during the feasting of the previous season. The name of the English leader is not given. Indeed, none of the heroes has been identified though many are praised by name in exalted terms for their honourable fulfilment of their pledges, their courage and loyalty to the death. The three hundred British warriors were wiped out, but not, it is claimed, before they had taken heavy toll of the English. It is the high tragedy of a small band doomed from the start and with no thought for the issue.

In *The Battle of Llwyfein Wood* Taliesin celebrates a victory of Owein, son of Urien, over the English.

Great blustering Flamddwyn shouted
'Are my hostages coming? Are they ready?'
Owein, preparing for battle, replied,
'They have not come, they are not ready' . . .
Urein, lord of Erechwydd, shouted:
'Let us carry our spearshafts over the mountain
And lift our faces above the ridge,
And raise our lances over men's heads,
And attack Flamddwyn in the midst of his host,
And slay both him and his companions.'

And in Taliesin's Death-song (*marwnad*) to Owein:

> It was nothing to Owein to slay Flamddwyn,
> He might have done it in his sleep.
> —A fine man in his gaudy harness
> Who gave horses to his dependents . . .
> The soul of Owein ap Urien,
> May the Lord have mind to his need.[7]

The poet expands nothing; he never reflects or allows for reflection—a series of brilliant brief statements, hyperbole against which criticism must remain silent, tragedy at a white heat, which carries the audience from one heroic image to another with never a moment's pause. It is rhetoric on the grand scale. Then, at the last, the inevitable static conventional motif—the solitary survivor who lives to tell the tale:

> Of the company of friends that went with us, sad it is that there returned but one man.

A large proportion of the poetry of the *Cynfeirdd* relates to persons who lived in the sixth century, most of whom are Britons of southern Scotland and north-western England. The leading subjects are the struggle of the Britons of southern Scotland and north-western England against the encroaching Saxons, the feuds of the Britons with one another, and the prowess of individuals. The heroes of the poems lived in the period of British independence after the departure of the Romans, and before the establishment of the Saxon kingdoms. These poems constitute our earliest record of the British Heroic Age, our earliest native records of British history.

In general the earliest British poetical traditions may be grouped into two Cycles of subjects. The first concerns the battle of Arderydd (cf. p. 64 above). The story of the battle is nowhere fully related, but it is the subject of numerous allusions in poems and triads. A group of poems of this Cycle but of later date are concerned with Myrddin (later Welsh *Merlin*),[8] who was evidently a North British warrior closely attached to Gwenddoleu, perhaps as his court bard. We gather from these poems that he loses his wits, doubtless in the battle,[9] and afterwards wanders in the forest of *Celyddon* ('Caledonia') for many years. The poems in question are the *Cyvoesi*, the *Ymddiddan* ('Dialogue') *of Myrddin and Taliesin*, composed before 1100, and the *Afallennau* ('The Apple Trees'), all late. In addition to these more or less coherent Cycles, and poems attributed to well-known *cynfeirdd*, a number of speech poems have survived, largely in three-line stanzas, and often in the form of monologues and dialogues, which have reference to heroes well-known from other sources, e.g. Arthur, Gereint, Tristan, Taliesin, but which appear to be later than the period to which these heroes can be assigned.

Certain poems in the manuscript known as *The Red Book of Hergest* claim from their contents to be the work of Llywarch Hen, 'Llywarch the Old'.[10] He is not mentioned by Nennius among the poets of this period, but there can be little doubt that he is a historical person and a contemporary of Urien, though the poems which claim to be by him are believed to belong to a later date, probably about the middle of the ninth century. They are therefore probably to be regarded as 'poems in character', dramatic monologues and dialogues. As always in Welsh poetry, the story, the situation, is indicated by allusion, never by narrative; so the course of events has to be inferred by the listener—a convention which, we may be sure, assumes that the audience would be familiar with the background.

The poems attributed to Llywarch Hen are without titles in the MS., but from the nature of their contents they may be divided into three Cycles.[11] The first relates to Urien of Rheged and his sons and members of his court, Taliesin and Llywarch himself. The background of these poems is the disastrous encounters with the English, and the poet describes the death of Urien and the desolation of his court, now a heap of rubble; the hearth, once a blaze of logs heating the cauldrons, now green with weed and covered with bugloss and dock leaves. Hound and falcon have gone, and the whole scene, once bright with rushlights, gay with the shouts of warriors when Urien and Owein were alive, has become a floor where pigs are rooting and birds are pecking about.

After the death of Urien, his head was borne away by his cousin; perhaps to secure it from desecration by the enemy, perhaps simply in accordance with ancient Celtic custom. And one of the most moving of the Old Welsh poems is the Lament, or keen, purporting to be chanted by Llywarch Hen over the severed head. It is composed in three-line stanzas each beginning with a slight variation of the refrain 'A head I carry', followed by a phrase sharply contrasting Urien in life:

A head I carry, close to my side,
Head of Urien, generous leader of hosts,
And on his white breast, a black carrion crow.
A head I carry . . .
Alive he was a refuge for the old.
A head I carry . . .
Whose war-bands patrolled vast territories
The head of much sung Urien, whose fame is far-scattered.

The poem proceeds by repetition and crescendo, and by stifled contrasting phrases to its rhetorical conclusion:

A head I hold up which once sustained me . . .
My arm is numb, my body trembles,
My heart breaks;
This head I cherish, formerly cherished me.

In the second Cycle we leave Urien of Rheged and his northern wars and the desolation of his hall after the owners have perished, for a different *milieu*. These poems relate to

Cynddylan, apparently a seventh-century ruler of Powys, whose home Pengwern, somewhere on the English Border, has been desolated, like that of Urien, by the English. Sir Ifor Williams has suggested that they formed the speech-poems of a lost saga, produced *c.* 850 in Powys, relating how the invading Angles and Saxons in their northward drive conquered Rheged, whence Llywarch, a solitary survivor, fled to Powys. Cynddylan's sister Heledd laments in a passionate keen the loss of Cynddylan and her other brothers, and bewails her solitary and wretched lot as she stands on the bare hill-top and looks down upon the smoking ruins of Shrewsbury, her former home.

> Grey-headed eagle of Pengwern,
> Tonight his claw hangs poised
> Greedy for the flesh I loved.

The compression is startling:

> Cynddylan's court is dark tonight,
> No fire, no bed;
> I weep awhile, then fall silent.

> Cynddylan's court is dark tonight,
> No fire, no songs—
> Tears wear away my cheeks.

> Cynddylan's court, it stabs me to see it,
> No roof, no fire;
> My lord-leader dead, myself alive.

And again:

> Wandering Heledd am I called.
> O God, to whom are given
> The lands of my brothers and their steeds?

> I look down from Wrekin Fort
> On the land of Freuer.
> Longing for the land of my brothers breaks my heart.

What we may call a third Cycle of poems purporting to be the work of Llywarch Hên are verses spoken partly in monologue by Llywarch himself, partly in dialogue with his son Gwen. In the latter, he urges the boy to give battle to the English invaders of Powys. There is also an elegy over the last of his twenty-four sons. Another poem is a pitiful lament on his own old age and inability to take part in the fight. While these poems are in the traditional style of the early poems described above, the *milieu* is different and seems to belong to a later age.

It is curious that Llywarch alone of the northern heroes has been transferred by the poet to the Welsh Border from his original *milieu* in the North. Yet his original connection with Urien is remembered by the horn which Urien is said to have given to Llywarch's son Gwen. Similarly the poet Taliesin, Urien's official bard, speaks of himself as singing to Brochfael, prince of Powys (cf. p. 101 above), and a saga was current about him in North Wales as early as the ninth century.[12] But these are only a few of the many transitions of the literature and traditions of the North to Wales, following on the annexation of the North British kingdoms by the Saxons, and the establishment of 'Merfyn Mawr from the north' in North Wales (cf. p. 72 above).

It is almost impossible for anyone who is not a native Welsh speaker, familiar with the strict Welsh metrical prosody,[13] to appreciate justly, still less to convey, the intellectual mastery of this tight-knit poetry, its concentrated brevity of phrase, its use of repetition and inversion and crescendo to achieve the climax of the final impact on the emotions which comes to us almost as a shock. This is, in fact, the effect at which the poet aims, for example, in the *Lament for Urien of Rheged* above, where the closing stanza achieves the finality of bereavement. To obtain his effect, the bard sacrifices reflection to emotion at a white-heat. Unfortunately no early Scottish poetry has survived.

The salient feature of all oral Celtic literature, Goedelic and Brythonic alike, is the fact that while from the earliest period we have practically no narrative poetry, and while narrative literature in both Irish and Welsh is embodied exclusively in prose form, little early Welsh prose has been preserved from before the twelfth century. From this period, however, we un-doubtedly have the original nucleus of a small number of prose sagas which are native in both form and substance, as can be seen by comparing them with Irish sagas on the one hand, and with contemporary English, French and Icelandic on the other. The most important are the four stories known as the *Mabinogion*. These are stories related in a highly polished style that have been transmitted from much earlier times by a native professional class of story-tellers, known as *cyfarwyddiaid* (sing. *cyfarwydd*). In the course of their long life through the centuries before they were recorded in medieval manuscripts these stories have lost nothing of their charm, though the actual course of the narrative is often confused and obscure. In polish and grace of style they may indeed have gained something under French influence, and medieval literary Irish influence is clearly visible too in some of the stories, notably *Branwen*.

In contrast to the strange blend of metrical rigidity and emotional tension of early Welsh poetry, the leisurely beauty and magic of the later prose seems to belong to another world. In our slender collection of medieval Welsh prose stories by far the best known is the beautiful quartet referred to above, and now known as *The Four Branches of the Mabinogion*.[14] The word *Mabinogi* means 'youth'; later it came to mean 'tales about youth', and finally, 'tales' in a general sense. The apocryphal gospel *De Infantia Jesu Christi* was translated in Wales in the fourteenth century as *Mabinogi Iesu Grist*. Perhaps it may be rendered 'Tales of the young'.

The *Four Branches* are also a contrast to the poems in another important respect. While the poems relate, or purport to relate, to contemporary people and events, especially in the North, the stories of the *Mabinogion* relate to traditional themes of the far past. The poems are realistic and direct for the most part, even when, as in the vaticinatory poems of Myrddin, they are often very obscure. This sense of reality is heightened by the use of direct speech, monologue or dialogue. In the prose, the background and the characters are different. The scene is laid for the most part in Wales, never in the 'North'; and the stories are essentially Welsh. On the other hand the prose is hardly ever realistic, and a sense of illusion is achieved by the simple and almost imperceptible transitions of the story from the world of reality to the world of the supernatural.

The 'Four Branches' are all located in Western Wales, and despite the close correspondence between many of the proper names of the ruling dynasties and those of Irish gods, there is no indication that the Welsh have borrowed from the Irish. The origin of the stories still remains a mystery. It is also a remarkable fact that there is no contact between the heroes of the *Mabinogi* and the Men of the North. Their worlds never meet. The style of the Welsh prose throughout is refined and courtly, and its delicacy suggests that the stories have been composed in their present form for recital in a lady's bower, even possibly for monastic 'recreation', and we can trace the result of a tardy influence of medieval literary standards penetrating these little Welsh societies.

Two other early Welsh prose stories are inspired by a keen antiquarian interest, and these recall heroes of the North. The earliest of them, *Kilhwch and Olwen*, believed to have been composed *c.* 1100, has its setting in the old heroic world; heroes and families and fragments of stories of the North mingle with those of Wales and Cornwall—a further reflection of the literary transfer already alluded to above. The framework is picaresque and consists largely of a long series of adventures which Arthur's nephew Kilhwch is obliged to undergo to win his bride Olwen, the daughter of the giant Yspadaddyn Penkawr; the climax of which is the shaving and tonsuring of the giant himself—perhaps a last satirical reference to the condemnation by the Roman Church of the traditional Celtic tonsure. The many allusions made, and the number of native stories referred to in the course of Kilhwch's adventures, practically amounts to a catalogue of lost native Welsh traditions. *Kilhwch and Olwen* more than any other prose tale enables us to form some estimate of the riches of earlier Welsh prose sagas, and of her lost literature.

One of the most delightful of the medieval Welsh prose sagas is the *Dream of Rhonabwy*, which, like *Kilhwch and Olwen*, again contains links with the old heroic families of the ancient north. The framework of the story is a dream of Rhonabwy, who is introduced to us as a member of the retinue of Madawg, prince of Powys, about the middle of the twelfth century. The dream presents us with a brilliant flashback to Arthur's camp at Rhyd-y-Groes, the large meadow at the ford over the River Severn, where today we can still see the ruins of the great Abbey of Strata Marcella; and it is tempting to believe that the saga was composed and written to celebrate the arrival *c.* 1195 of the last of the Welsh princes, Owain Cyfeiliog, to end his days in this abbey. It is probable that the story as we have it was composed by one of the brothers in the abbey. Three other medieval Welsh prose stories are again attached to King Arthur, and although all three reappear in the French romances, the setting and the original nucleus have been shown to be undoubtedly native Welsh.

Dr Thomas Parry has briefly outlined how these romances differ from the older type of prose narratives discussed above.[15] Now the incidents are centred round one man, rather than relating to various families, or to a group of people. The character and function of Arthur have changed. He is no longer an active and daring chieftain, but the ruler of a court of chivalry at Caerleon from which the hero sets out on his journey and to which he returns. The adventures of the heroes are wholly unlocalised, in this a sharp contrast to those of the Welsh tales in which the ruling princes are firmly located at well-known centres in Wales. The whole atmosphere has changed from the world as we know it, in spite of its magic and transformations, to a world of wholly artificial standards and the atmosphere of the world of chivalry.

The late story of *Lludd and Llevelys* is believed to represent a purely native tradition, free from Norman French influence, and harking back to pseudo-historical native themes. But by far the best of these stories of pseudo-history is *The Dream of Macsen Wledig*, a story of thirteenth-century date, in which it is related how the Roman Emperor, Magnus Maximus, came to Britain in response to a dream, and married a noble British bride, Elen Luyddog, 'Elen of the Hosts'.[16] In style and finish the *Dream of Macsen* shows perhaps the Welsh *cyfarwyd's* narrative power at its best, and it is said to be most effective when recited. It gives us something of an insight into the attitude of the Welsh story-teller to history, for he has expended his finest art on the Roman emperor who centuries earlier had lived in North Wales, and whose departure with Roman troops was believed to have brought Roman Britain to an end. In Cornwall too he lived on in tradition as *Mytern* (Welsh *macteyrn*) *Macsen,* 'Maximus the Prince', in the medieval Cornish verse miracle play *Beunans Meriasek,* 'The Life of Saint Meriasek'.[17] Here, however, the hagiological tradition has transformed him into a tyrant who persecutes the saint.

Unfortunately no collections of British sagas have been preserved in the North, though we know from allusions in literature of a later date, especially in the *Lives of the Saints,* that an extensive saga literature must have been in wide circulation in the North in early times.[18] In particular St Kentigern, the patron saint of Glasgow and of Strathclyde generally, is the focus of a whole cycle of saga literature. Indeed the anonymous twelfth-century *Life* of the saint has all the features of oral prose saga. The *Life of St Cadoc*,[19] though written *c.* 1100 in South Wales, is a great collection of saga and folklore, part of which relates to the saint's sojourn in southern Scotland, and is especially interesting for its incorporation (ch. 26) of a legend of a Pictish robber chief, Cau of Pictavia, whose collar-bone the saint accidentally digs up while excavating the foundations for a new monastery. Cau must have been a formidable raider, for his collar-bone is big enough for a man on horseback to ride through. He was evidently the centre of a whole cycle of sagas, for the same source states (ch. 27) that he was the father of Gildas *scriptor optimus*; and the twelfth-century *Life of St Gildas de Rhuys* claims that Cau belonged to Strathclyde and was the father of Gildas the saint. He is also referred to as the father of several sons associated with King Arthur in medieval Welsh tradition. In the *Dream of Rhonabwy* his son Gwarthegyt seems to be Arthur's chief councillor, while in *Kilhwch and Olwen* nineteen sons of Cau are listed as present at Arthur's court.

Many of the most interesting adventures of the Irish hero Cuchulainn, known to us from Irish sagas, take place in Scotland, and seem to be of Pictish origin. The two queens, Scathach and Aoife are natives of Alba, doubtless Pictavia, while the adventures of Emer[20] seem to belong to the same *milieu*. Many references in medieval Scottish literature, from Wyntoun onwards, speak of stories of marvel relating to Macbeth,[21] and other early Scottish Chronicles refer all too briefly to traditional sagas relating to the early kings.

One of the most widely practised forms of intellectual activity in traditional Welsh literature is the mnemonic convention of the Triad, by which various classes of people, events, etc., having as is suggested some common characteristic, are grouped in sets of three. They are like miniature catalogues of the repertoires of the Welsh story-tellers, by which heroes,

stories, events, etc., can be readily set in their appropriate context, a kind of oral library catalogue. As an example we may
refer to Triad 24:

Three Battle-Leaders of the Island of Britain:
Selyf son of Cynan Garwyn,
And Urien son of Cynfarch,
And Afaon son of Taliesin.

We have already referred to 'Three Futile Battles of Britain' in
Triad 84, one of which was 'fought for a lark's nest' (cf. p. 64
above).

Sometimes the rhetorical effect is heightened and the
mnemonic value strengthened by contrasting juxtaposed Triads.
Triad 29 names:

Three Faithful War-Bands of the Island of Britain:
The War-Band of Cadwallawn son of Cadfan who were
with him seven years in Ireland . . .
And the War-Band of Gafran son of Aeddan, who went
to sea for their lord;
And the War-Band of Gwenddolau son of Ce(i)diaw at
Ar(f)derydd, who continued the battle for a fortnight and
a month after their lord was slain.

As opposed to these we have (Triad 30):

Three Faithless War-Bands of the Island of Britain,
The War-Band of Goronwy Peuyr of Penllyn . . . and the
War-Band of Gwrgi and Peredur, who abandoned their
lord at Caer Greu, etc.[22]

The Triads have much to tell us of the heroes of the North. In
this they resemble the *Englynion y Beddau*, 'Verses of the Graves',
which constitute an inventory of the graves of the heroes of
Welsh sagas. The origin of neither *Triads* nor *Beddau* is known.

Both are undoubtedly ancient, though the people mentioned belong to widely different periods, and both give us some idea of the great wealth of saga which was once current in Britain, but is now lost. Of the eighty warriors listed in the *Beddau*, the stories of hardly twenty are now known to us, and these are of mythological figures from the *Mabinogi* and saga heroes of the sixth and seventh centuries whom we have already met in the North, including Rhydderch Hael, Owein ap Urien, and Cynan ap Clydno Eidin. It is again significant of the transference of early northern traditions to Wales, that the graves are almost all located in Wales, chiefly in North Wales.

CHAPTER VII

Art

THE EARLY CHRISTIAN inscribed stone monuments are among the principal material remains in Britain from the period between the close of the Roman Occupation and the establishment of the Saxon kingdoms. Their chief extension is along the western seaboard, especially on the peninsulas, the greatest concentrations being those of the Devon-Cornish peninsula, Cornwall especially; Dyfed, or the wider Pembrokeshire; Lleyn, or the Caernarvonshire peninsula; the Isle of Man; and the British area of south-western Scotland, especially the groups at Whithorn and Kirkmadrine.

Plate 34

These inscriptions are the earliest messages left to us in direct speech from our ancestors, and Britain is the only province of the Roman Empire in which inscriptions on the early Christian monuments appear in the native as well as in the Latin language.[1] A number are bilingual, being cut both in the Latin alphabet and in the old Celtic alphabet known as 'ogam' (cf. p. 99 above). The ogam inscriptions of southern Britain are in the Irish form of Celtic, and are found in Devon and Cornwall, Wales, and the Isle of Man. In the western peninsulas of Wales, the population in the fifth and sixth centuries was largely bilingual, i.e. both Welsh- and Irish-speaking. The individual inscriptions are difficult to date with precision, but the ogam alphabet, even if invented in the fourth century, is not likely to have come into general use so early. All are Christian memorial monuments, but they tell us little beyond the name and patronymic of the individual commemorated. The inscriptions in Wales are mostly in the Latin alphabet, but 40 are in ogam, and occasionally both are found on the same stone (cf. p. 41 above). The ogam alphabet on a number of Pictish inscriptions (cf. p. 56 above) resembles a type current in Ireland in the eighth century, and they are generally known as 'scholastic ogams'. They are probably not earlier in Pictavia than the eighth or even the ninth century (cf. p. 56 above).

In contrast to her rich literary tradition and many inscriptions on stone, Wales is relatively poor in material of high artistic merit in our period. No early illuminated manuscripts have come down to us. The manuscript of St Augustine's *De Trinitate*, now in Cambridge, which is known to have been transcribed by Ieuan ap Sulien of Llanbadarn Fawr at the request of his father, Bishop Sulien of St David's, in the second half of the eleventh century, contains several beautiful Celtic initials in vermilion, green, black and yellow. These illuminations are almost certainly the work of Ieuan himself, who supplied the fine Celtic illuminations of the Psalter of his brother Rhygyfarch (Ricemarch).

Though the quality of the art of stone sculpture in Wales is poor by comparison with the best Irish and Northumbrian examples, Wales possesses a wealth of stone crosses, sculptured both in relief and also free-standing. Both forms are believed to have developed in Britain and in southern Scotland under influences from Ireland and the Continent. Indeed, in both stone inscriptions and stone sculpture, as in other cultural matters, Scotland south of the Forth–Clyde line may be looked upon as a unity with southern and western Britain, while the artistic affinities of Argyll are with Ireland, as we should expect. In the British areas the sculptor's art has developed chiefly in relief on cross-slabs and on free-standing crosses. The art of Cornwall, a poor country, though numerically rich in stone crosses, is not of high quality. The Isle of Man developed a great wealth and originality of motifs at a later date, partly under Viking inspiration. The Pictish sculptures, which belong to a different artistic world, are the supreme achievement, in sculpture in Britain in our period.

Fig. 19

Fig. 19. Welsh fish. Illumination at the top of folio 76 of the Psalter composed c. *1079 by Rhygyfarch (Ricemarch), son of Sulien, Bishop of St David's, Pembrokeshire. The illuminations are the work of his brother Ieuan (John), the colours used being red, yellow and green (after Lawlor)*

The memorial stones from Wales and western Britain afford a valuable standard of the culture of our period among these western Celtic peoples, who, after the departure of the Romans, retained a conservative and, it would seem, relatively high grade of civilisation as compared with eastern Britain.[2] Moreover, the western inscriptions reflect new influences from Gaul operating on our western seaboard. This is seen, not only in the new range of proper names, such as Martin and Paulinus, which became popular in Gaul in the fourth and fifth centuries, but also in the use of formulae current in Gaul at this time, which had superseded the Roman, and even in the introduction of the wider Continental (e.g. Byzantine) formulae and fashions of epigraphy.[3] Occasionally in western Wales the official status of the deceased is specified (cf. p. 38 above). A stone in Llangian churchyard in the Lleyn peninsula, Caernarvonshire, commemorates a doctor: '*Meli medici fili Martini j(a)cet*'— 'The stone of Melus the doctor, son of Martin'.[4] But such references to the profession of the deceased are rare in the Christian inscriptions of Britain, though not uncommon on the Continent.

One interesting family group of local Pembrokeshire magnates can be reconstructed from four stones in a relatively small area. A pillar-stone in Llandeilo churchyard (no. 313) commemorates a certain Andagellus, son of Cavetus, in both Latin and ogam letters; another pillar-stone (no. 314) in the same churchyard commemorates in Latin Coimagnus, son of Cavetus; a pillar-stone (no. 345), also in Latin, at Maenchlochog commemorates Curcagnus, son of Andagellus. Here we have commemorated three generations from one family. One stone (no. 183) from Pentrefoelas in Denbighshire of the fifth or sixth century was probably erected in association with a Christian cemetery, and for this we shall find parallels in southern Scotland. A few bear the formula *hic jacit* before the name of the deceased, and occasionally Christian symbols are inscribed. The majority take the form of rough pillar-stones and slabs.

Most of the Welsh stones decorated with crosses, whether in the round as free-standing monuments or in relief on a shaped slab, date from the seventh to ninth centuries. The more elaborate are decorated over the entire surface with typical Celtic designs in interlace, knot-work, and various geometrical designs, both curvilinear and rectilinear, frequently arranged in panels. The technique and the planning and execution of the design are of a high order, and the intricate geometrical designs are adapted to their panels with masterly competence, and generally executed with flawless precision. Human figures and animals are relatively rare, but occur occasionally on the lowest panels, as is frequently the case with the little realistic genre scenes on the Irish high crosses. Most of the Welsh crosses are flat, but pillar-crosses are not unknown, the most famous being the so-called Eliseg's Pillar[5] with its long but much defaced inscription (cf. p. 44 above).

Cornwall has preserved nine inscriptions on stone, written in Roman capitals and dating from the fifth and sixth centuries, as well as a few which bear ogam inscriptions.[6] The most interesting of the sixth-century inscriptions is the so-called 'Castle Dore stone',[7] near Fowey. The inscription appears to read *'Drustaus* [or *Cirusius*] *hic jacit Cunomori filius'*—'Here lies Drusta(n) [or Cirusius] the son of Cunomorus', and

Plate 35

Cunomorus was identified with King Mark at an early date. It possibly commemorates the legend of Tristan (*Drustan*), the lover of Iseult, King Mark's wife. The earliest dateable examples of the wheel-headed cross sculptured in the round are thought to be Irish work of the tenth century; and from the tenth century we have a number of crosses with Hiberno-Saxon ornament closely resembling those of South Wales, from which, indeed, they are believed to be derived.[8] The most elaborate is the Cardynham Cross[9] near Bodmin, with a beautifully carved and designed head, while the Sancreed Cross, probably contemporary, bears on its head a rude crucifixion.[10]

Plate 36

The Isle of Man has more than 90 carved stones, mostly upright slabs with incised crosses, of which very few are decorated. Three bear inscriptions in Latin, one of them of the Welsh type, and four are in ogam characters. Among the most interesting is an incised slab from Maughold, probably of the eighth century. It bears a circle enclosing the conventional 'marigold' design, Mediterranean in origin, surrounded by a difficult Latin inscription; and below the circle are two little crosses of rare early type.[11] The most elaborate and the most delicate and accomplished early Manx sculpture is an incised slab,[12] assigned to the early ninth century,[13] found on the site of an early Celtic chapel on the Calf of Man. It represents a Crucifixion, and is of unique design. Christ hangs on the Cross, elaborately dressed, with long hair parted in the middle and forked beard. His feet are uncrossed and hang straight down, and the feet and right hand—the left is broken away—are pierced by large nails. The head is upright, the eyes are wide open.

Plate 38

Fig. 20

Plate 37

Of special historical interest is a cross slab bearing the inscription: *Crux Guriat*[14] (cf. p. 72 above), now standing in Maughold churchyard. Except for a shallow beading and heavily protruding bosses, the groundwork is quite plain; but a great deal of skilled cutting away of the original stone was

Plate 38

necessary to leave these bosses free. We shall find a similar highly skilled technique on some of the best Pictish sculpture. Whether this was the tombstone of Guriat, related to Merfyn Frych (p. 72 above), remains uncertain, but the quality of the workmanship and the original position of the stone in relation to Maughold suggest that the Guriat commemorated here was at least a person of importance, and except in Merfyn's family the name is rare.

The earliest series of Christian inscribed stones which we have been following up the west coast of southern Britain continues into the part of southern Scotland which was racially, linguistically, and culturally akin to the Britons who extended from the Clyde to Land's End. The surviving early Christian memorials in southern Scotland are not numerous, but at least two of these seem to indicate Christian cemeteries which have disappeared. The famous Catstone at Kirkliston,[15] about six miles west of Edinburgh (cf. p. 40 above), is a large unhewn boulder, about four and a half feet above ground, bearing in debased Roman capitals the inscription: *In (h)oc tumulo jacit Vetta f Victi* (In this tumulus lies Vetta, son of Victus)—a typical formula of British Christian inscriptions. The stone stands in an ancient cemetery which was enclosed by a rough-hewn stone wall encompassing 51 stone-lined graves arranged in rows in Christian fashion. The monument is unique in that it still stands *in situ* in the midst of its graves; but the comparable inscribed slab at Yarrowkirk in Selkirkshire, already described (p. 40 above), was also associated with a Christian cemetery.

The chief concentration of early sculptured and inscribed stones, however, is in Scotland's remote south-west peninsula, and ranges from the fifth to the seventh century. Three at Kirkmadrine in the Rinns of Galloway, and two at Whithorn are clearly memorials to Christians, and must have stood in the cemeteries of ancient church sites. All of these except the earliest bear Christian symbols in imitation of Continental

Plate 9

Fig. 20. Early Manx cross from Maughold, Isle of Man (after Kinvig). Probably early eighth century. Note the early 'marigold' design inside the circle, and the two archaic and rare types of crosses below

usage. The oldest stone at Whithorn, the famous 'Latinus stone', a roughly squared pillar dating from about the middle of the fifth century, is the earliest Christian memorial in Scotland, and is interpreted: 'We praise thee, Lord, Latinus aged thirty-five and his daughter aged four. The grandson of Barrovius set up this memorial here.' The famous St Peter stone, a squared stone pillar with an incised cross in a double incised circle, bears the inscription: *Loci Petri Apustoli.* A *locus* is a place dedicated in honour of a saint, and the cross was originally found by the roadside not far from the monastic site of Whithorn, and is probably of seventh-century date. Three of the Kirkmadrine stones belong to the sixth century, but the most interesting, a memorial to three priests, is ascribed to the fifth century.

Fig. 21

Fig. 22

The art of the early Christian monuments of Argyll is wholly
Irish in character. There survive on Iona two wheel-headed
crosses, dedicated, one to St John, the other to St Martin

Plate 57   a relatively rare dedication in early Britain after the one in

*Fig. 21. The 'St Peter's stone', Whithorn.
It formerly stood beside the road to the south.
Probably seventh century (after Radford)*

Canterbury referred to by Bede (*H.E.* I, 26). A number of fragments of some five other crosses are also to be found on Iona. The two surviving crosses stand on a high base, and like most of the Irish high crosses are free-standing, the arms pierced by a ring—a type confined in Scotland to Argyll and the Hebrides, and assigned to the ninth and tenth centuries.

As though in compensation for the total absence of written literature dating back to the period of the independent Pictish kingdom, we have in Scotland north of the Forth a vast picture gallery of Pictish art, now surviving chiefly in stone sculpture of superb and mature quality. These sculptured monuments, of which there are over 100 in existence, stretch from the Firth of Forth to the Shetlands, and from the east coast to the Hebrides; but their chief concentration is in the east, along the coast and the river valleys, and they constitute the distinctive art of the Picts. As Mr Stevenson has admirably expressed it: 'To stand in front of one of these sculptured stones is to come as close as is now possible to the Picts. For not only are they vivid works of art, but they are what chiefly survives of Pictish sculpture.' [16] They are indeed the national monuments of the Picts.

The sculptures occur both incised and in relief, but never free-standing. The classification originally formulated by Joseph Anderson in 1892[17] has been accepted in principle by all succeeding scholars, and with some additional details by R. B. K. Stevenson may be expressed as follows:

Class I. Rude, unshaped boulders bearing incised symbols, chiefly of geometrical but partly of animal form, dating approximately from the sixth to the eighth centuries A.D.

Class II. Dressed slabs bearing sculpture in relief—the figure of the cross, symbols and other figures, and Celtic ornament—generally on a carefully shaped monument. Although Christian iconography occurs, the Crucifixion is never presented, but naturalistic animals and scenes of human life are common. They range from the seventh to the ninth centuries.

Fig. 22. Roughly squared tombstone, found in the old burial ground of Kirkmadrine, Wigtown, commemorating three 'chief priests'. Fifth century (after Radford)

Class III. Similar sculptured slabs, overlapping with Class II designs, but without symbols, later in date than those of Class II and continuing to the twelfth century. Here the variety is much greater, and the upright slab is now of great size. With Class III, in so far as the monuments show close

relationship with Northumbria and Ireland and are not dis-
tinctively Pictish in design, we shall not in general be concerned
here.

Class I is unique, the symbols being unknown in the art of
any other country. Their origin and the purpose of the carvings
are totally unknown. This is illustrated in a striking way by the
most abstract of the 'symbols', which, together with the so-
called 'swimming elephants', are also the commonest. They
take the form of a crescent, with or without elaborate internal

Fig. 23

Fig. 30

Fig. 23. *Inscribed Pictish symbol stone,
Kinblethmont, Angus* (after *Wainwright*)

Fig. 24. *Incised slab with Pictish symbols, Dun-
nichen, Angus* (after *Cruden*)

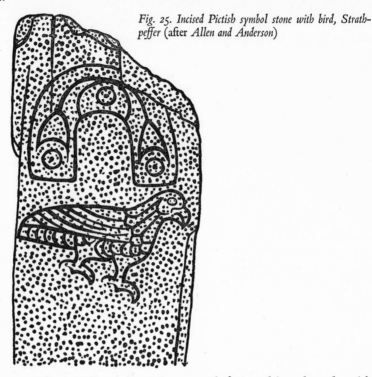

Fig. 25. Incised Pictish symbol stone with bird, Strath-peffer (after Allen and Anderson)

curvilinear decoration, intersected by a hinged rod with
equivalent arms, commonly ending in a floreated terminal; two
circles joined like spectacles, intersected by a doubly hinged rod
with leaf-like terminals; a serpent intersected by a similar rod;
and various modifications of these, especially the rod, often
alone. Many of the incised objects, not necessarily symbols, are
easily recognisable—mirror and comb, fish, goose, eagle, sea-
horse, mermaid, and a large number of various animals, such
as the bull, the boar, the stag, the wolf, all depicted in a completely stereotyped form, but with stylised anatomical details
indicating their salient physical features, and the characteristics
of their natures. The Brandsbutt boulder and the Golspie slab
have both symbols and an ogam inscription.

Fig. 23

Fig. 24

Figs. 24–26

Fig. 27

Plate 42

The originality and beauty of the work is matched by an impressive mastery of execution. While sandstone is most commonly used, many of these curvilinear designs are incised in granite, that most intractable form of stone. Yet they are for the most part executed with unhesitating assurance and perfection. Only a people with a high standard of material culture could have produced the tools, supported the highly trained and skilled class of artists and technical experts, and financed so great a number of surviving examples—the immortal memorial of a great nation.

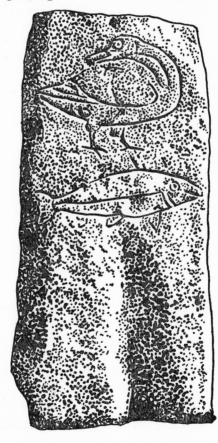

Fig. 26. Inscribed Pictish symbol stone with goose and fish (note the slight misplacement of the dorsal fin). Easterton of Roseisle, Elgin (after Cruden)

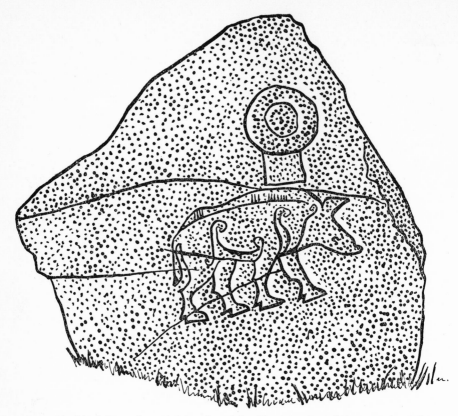

Fig. 27. *Slab of hard slate with inscribed Pictish symbol and boar, Knocknagael, Inverness-shire. The stone stands on the edge of a field by the roadside about 3 miles south of Inverness railway station* (after *Allen and Anderson*)

Fig. 28
Plate 29
Fig. 29

Fig. 30, 31

We cannot even guess at their origin. A few examples of these designs have survived on ivory, silver and bronze objects. We have a record of a bronze disc from the Laws, Monifieth, Angus, as well as of a number of silver chains with symbols on their terminal links, and a silver leaf-shaped plate. Apart from the technique of the carvings, the mastery of line-drawing suggests strongly that what is before us is the fine flower of the teaching of many an artist's studio; but the period for development is extremely restricted. Several caves have numerous inscribed symbols and other pictures on their walls. The dating is complicated through some caves having also large numbers of crosses and *graffiti* incised on their walls, and these, with the traditions of their occupation by early Celtic saints, such as St Serf at Dysart and St Constantine at Fifeness, suggest a long, continuous history of habitation. Apart from the crosses, the art of the caves is for the most part that of the symbol stones. Its purpose is as unknown here as is that of the boulders and the slabs. The drawing, moreover, is very uneven in quality. Some suggest an artist's 'trial pieces'; but a fair proportion of the figures are of fine quality, both in their grace and naturalism. The cave art in general deserves more careful study than it has received hitherto. The Wemyss caves (cf. p. 93) make good homes.

The number and variety of symbol forms, a dozen or more different types, on monuments of Class I and Class II, used over and over again, suggest that they were probably in use for a considerable time, and they cannot have had their origin in Christian iconography, for stones of Class I never appear with

Fig. 29. Silver leaf-shaped plate with Pictish symbols inscribed, Large, Fife (after Anderson)

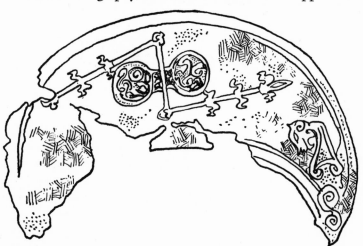

Fig. 28. Inscribed Pictish symbols on obverse of bronze plate found at the Laws, Monifieth, Angus (after Anderson)

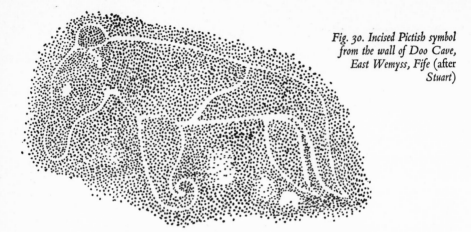

Fig. 32

Christian symbols except in the caves, though they are frequently associated with them on stones of Class II. The pagan motifs, such as the mermaid and the centaur, belong, not to local paganism, but to the late Classical designs of the Mediterranean world, and we may seek some of the strange animal motifs in the same menagerie of unnatural natural history as we find in the later bestiaries.

The symbols are very stereotyped in character, and the margin within which variation is permissible is very narrow, as Stevenson has shown in his diagram of the development of the

Fig. 31. Incised drawings and symbols on the wall of Jonathan's cave, East Weymss, Fife (after Stuart

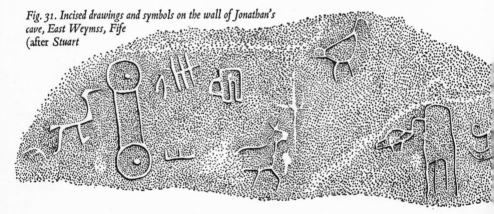

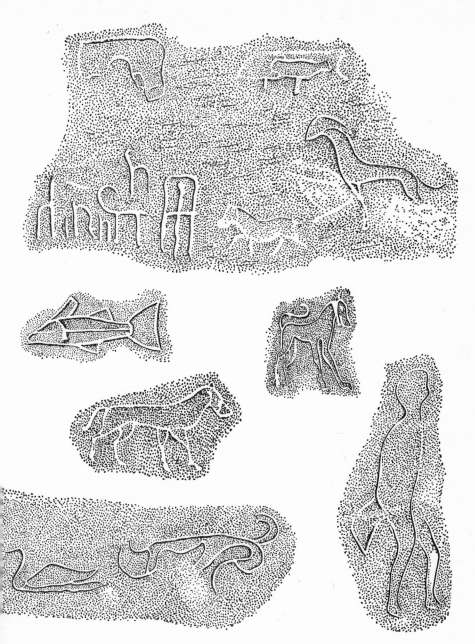

Fig. 32. Centaur with axes or hammers. Pictish inscribed sculptured cross-slab, Glamis, Angus (after Diack)

crescent.[18] This is particularly noticeable in the Type I animals, of which the special home is around Inverness. There was evidently a 'type' of each animal which all sculptors had to observe. This is particularly marked in the 'elephant', and in the series of completely conventional Burghead bulls; a 'correct' iconography seems to have prevailed also in regard to the duck and eagle. These Class I animal 'symbols' are quite distinct from those of Class II, which are not only a different range of animals, but seem largely to lack the element of symbolism and to favour naturalism. This stereotyped character of Class I is not, however, divorced from naturalism but based on it; the lobes and internal lines of the best animal and bird sculptures articulate the muscles of the animals, and the lie of the feathers and wing pinions of the birds. In fact a sculptor's animal 'alphabet' developed, accompanied by a system of short-hand.

Fig. 33
The spirited little horse of the Inverurie boulder of Class I springs to life—the Platonic idea of a young horse in full career, its speed emphasised by the three rigid upright hairs, suggesting a flying mane or crest, identical with one on the horse incised on the wall of King's Cove, Arran. The same symbolic 'short-hand alphabet' of three or four upright hairs like wire is used to denote hair on the Burghead bulls.

The great majority of incised symbol stones are found north of the Mounth, but the original centre of distribution is disputed. Mrs Curle points out that the stones of the best quality are in Orkney. Anderson and Allen favoured Aberdeenshire, and Mr Stevenson also favours Aberdeenshire, where most of the 'swimming elephants' occur. Mrs Henderson[19] has recently brought forward evidence in favour of the head of the Great Glen in Inverness-shire, and the shores of the Moray and Dornoch Firths. While in the extreme north the symbol stones are almost all coastal, there are hardly any Class I stones along

Fig. 33. Horse, Inverurie, Aberdeenshire. Incised slab of red granite. The muscles emphasise the forward movement of the horse in action.

the coasts from Aberdeen to Inverness. Their spread, which is from north to south, is by the main river valleys, of the Spey, the Don, and the Urie, and over the Mounth passes to the kingdoms of the Southern Picts; and one can follow the symbols on their route. Only the prestige and power of a great ruler could account for the high quality and wide distribution of these Class I symbol stones from Shetland to the Forth, from the North Sea to the outer Hebrides, with an outlier at Anworth in Kirkcudbrightshire. It is natural, with Mrs Henderson, to connect this development of the symbol stones on the Moray-shire coast and the Voray and Dornoch Firths with the centre of power of the Northern Picts under Brude mac Maelchon in the sixth century, at the head of the Great Glen, giving easy access as it does to both the northern and the Western Isles. The penetration of the symbols through the passes of the Mounth to Angus, and their combination with a fresh and living art and a quite new technique in Class II, may well be connected with the passing of the supreme Pictish power from the Northern to the Southern Picts.

The curious paradox about Pictish animal art is that the most stereotyped forms appear to precede the splendid world of naturalistic animals characteristic of Pictish art of Class II, the art of the Southern Picts in their chief area around the Tay Valley during the middle of the eighth century. During this period and in this area the technique has changed from incised art on undressed stone to relief sculpture on a carefully dressed and shaped slab. The slab very frequently, but by no means always, takes the form of an upright memorial stone bearing a cross on one side, and secular scenes, designs or symbols on the reverse, the scenes being in a purely naturalistic style.

Plate 43

Some of the slabs are filled in with interlace and scroll- and knot-work comparable with contemporary Irish art, and ultimately reminiscent of metal work, as at Aberlemno and Nigg.

Some have large protruding bosses covered with interlace, again as at Nigg. Human beings, except horsemen, are comparatively rare on the cross slabs. The lady riding her horse side-saddle on the slab at Hilton of Cadboll is the only female figure represented in Pictish sculpture. But the most remarkable feature of these Class II stones is the large-scale 'narrative scenes', often on the reverse face of the slab from that bearing the cross, as at Aberlemno. The artist is at his most brilliant with horses and horsemen, hunting scenes and battle pieces, or the pageantry of battle. The rapid movement and exuberance, coupled with the unerring drawing of the figures, well proportioned and to scale, the masterly composition of the picture and the illusion of a living scene are in striking contrast to the austere, even hieratic designs and execution of the symbol stones, and resemble a great manuscript page or sheet of tapestry. Yet we are still in the world of symbol stones, for these are found on the same 'page' of the slabs as those living scenes, for example on the slab of Dunfallandy. On the back of the Aberlemno cross and on the slab of Hilton of Cadboll symbols occupy the upper half of the register. The latter cross is believed to date from *c.* 800.

Among the rarer but highly interesting groups of Pictish figure sculpture are some rectangular slabs found in Perthshire at Murthly, Meigle, and Dull[20]—all in the valley of the Tay. They are thin slabs, covered with sculpture on one side only, and were probably designed to form a frieze of a building, whether internal, or external. Meigle indeed stands out as pre-eminent in both range and technique. In the little slab figured by Cruden,[21] mastery in relief art creates the illusion, and indeed almost achieves the reality, of free-standing sculpture in the round. This is not easy to illustrate in a picture, but is very marked when one is in front of the sculpture and can insert one's finger-tips behind the outline which is deeply undercut. At Meigle too the sculptor has achieved the sculptor's ideal, transforming the natural and immediate into the permanent in the

Plate 44

Plate 46

Plates 45, 47

Plate 48

Plate 40

Fig. 34

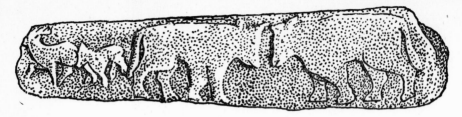

Fig. 34. Fighting bulls. Pictish sculptured slab, Meigle (after Cruden)

two fighting bulls, terrifying in their restrained power, forever in static preparation for battle.

A still more remarkable feature of the technique of these little Meigle slabs is the relationship of the figures to their background and also to the frame which borders the panel. The whole sculpture is in some examples executed in three receding planes. This form of technique is especially developed in the simpler themes, such as the small panels which contain pairs of heraldically facing animals. The method adopted by the sculptor was as follows: first he outlined the figures and the frame on his flat panel. Next he cut out the groundwork as far as the frame, which was reserved to outline his picture, leaving the figures standing out in relief beyond it. He then cut back all the rest of the groundwork except the frame. The figures thus stand forward of the frame, which merely, but very skilfully, now serves to define the field, and the whole creates the illusion of free-standing sculpture—or, if we prefer, of two animals confronting one another in a fenced field.

I may perhaps interpolate here that among the many excellent studies of the art of the Picts relatively little attention has been devoted to the technique of the sculpture. Yet much is to be learnt from the varying methods by which the sculptor approaches his surface and his field, and the way he handles his tools, perhaps also from the range of tools at his disposal. It may be suggested, therefore, that a special study might profitably be made of the sculptures from the point of view of the stone-mason's technique.

Some later outstanding monuments of the Class III phase, which are free from symbol designs yet of wholly Pictish provenance and artistic *milieu,* deserve a fuller study than is possible here. The most important is the St Andrews sarcophagus shrine—probably the shrine of St Regulus, the founder of the early Church—in the cathedral burial ground at St Andrews, where the shrine now stands. This sarcophagus is ascribed to the first half of the tenth century.[22] It is incomplete, but must originally have been a little less than 6 feet long, 3 feet wide, and 4 feet high. One of the longer panels contains a representation of David as shepherd, hunter, and lion slayer. The scene is naturalistic and in high relief, the principal figures standing out beyond the frame in the manner described above. The cross slabs at both Nigg and Crosston at Aberlemno[23] also represent David as shepherd and hunter. Pictish art is hunters' art, and the affinities with Sassanian and Assyrian art are evident in the Assyrian type of lion and lion hunt, the monkeys and gryphon, and the generous use of vegetation, unfamiliar in Scottish art.[24] These Eastern influences are important, despite the purely Celtic character of the decoration in the smaller panels, where the raised bosses recall the Iona crosses. Although most of the 'Oriental themes' are found also in Ireland, the art of Pictavia is never Irish art. The tall cross slabs, unknown in Northumbria, and little used latterly in Ireland, remain universally in Pictavia, while the free-standing cross of Ireland and Northumbria and Argyll is virtually unknown in Pictavia. Even the cross itself tends to be treated decoratively. In a Christian country, open to strong Christian influences from west, south and east, which have left their record on the history, the literature, the intellectual life and the architecture of Cruithentuach, the art of the Cruithne or Picts had its birth and continued to live its own national life in a world apart.

The high achievement of Pictish art has been more widely recognised and appreciated since the discovery of the St

Plate 49

Plate 50

Ninian's treasure, referred to above (p. 96). These objects are among the most beautiful found in Scotland. They were deposited in circumstances quite unknown, probably during the eighth century, perhaps under Viking pressure (as suggested above). There are 27 items, and their quality and variety is dazzling. All the objects are of silver, some gilded, and all of a high level of excellence in art and execution: richly chased brooches inset with semi-precious stones, silver cones and chapes of equally fine workmanship, conventionally decorated, and most important of all, seven bowls of rare shapes ornamented with geometrical and interlacing designs finely executed by means of a variety of tools. One bowl has a special interest as being apparently of east Mediterranean origin. Most interesting of all is a hanging bowl, the latest and most northerly example in the British Isles of this much debated class.

Plates 51–54

One of the bowls, perforated at the base, may have been a strainer for Communion wine, and a single-pronged instrument and a spoon may also have been part of the Communion plate. The most striking piece in the collection is a dog's head attaching the handle to the bowl of the spoon. It is startling in its realism. The staring eyes are of blue glass, the protruding tongue greedily licks the bowl of the spoon, the ears are laid back flat to the skull, as is the habit with a hungry dog. This intimate little object is the only example of naturalism in the art of this collection, but the stylised and unhesitating treatment of the muscles indicates a tradition of animal

Plate 54

modelling already stereotyped, and so the St Ninian's dog is first cousin to the animals of the Pictish symbol stones. Its naturalism is of a different order from that of the animals in a

Plate 55

hunting frieze on the silver bowl in the Traprain Law treasure, where between the legs of a hyena chasing a ram while a second

Fig. 35

hyena leaps on another ram's back, we watch a little hare crouching on the ground, its ears laid back, as it quietly washes its paw.

Fig. 35. Part of the design on the Traprain Law silver dish (cf. Plate 55)

The fullest collection of the early inscribed and sculptured stones of southern Scotland is the one in the Museum of Whithorn Priory, Wigtownshire. The Kirkmadrine stones are collected in the open west porch of the ancient parish church of Kirkmadrine. Of Pictish sculptures the best local collection is in a small but admirably arranged museum at Meigle, Perthshire. Others are at St Vigean's near Arbroath, Angus. The St Andrews sarcophagus and other early Christian and medieval sculptures are in the small museum in the Cathedral grounds at St Andrews. An extensive collection of original sculptures, and a large series of casts of others not in the collection, are in the National Museum of Antiquities, Edinburgh. A great many of these Pictish stones, however, are still in or near their original position. With Perth as a centre, in a few days almost all the incised and sculptured monuments of the southern Picts can easily be visited by train, bus, and by short walks.

CHAPTER VIII

The Church

THE EXACT DATE or the circumstances of the introduction of Christianity into Britain are unknown, but
both Tertullian and Origen refer to it in a manner which
implies that it was already established by the second century,[1]
and we have well attested traditions of three martyrdoms which
took place in Britain before 260.[2] The three British bishops
summoned to the Councils of Arles in 314 and Rimini in
359 imply an organised British Church,[3] and it doubtless had
a continuous history, for we hear repeatedly in the correspondence of St Athanasius and St Hilary of Poitiers of the keen
interest of the Britons in the affairs of the Western Church.
Even after the withdrawal of the Romans from Britain, Pope
Celestine evidently regarded this land as the stronghold of
the Pelagian heresy;[4] for Prosper of Aquitaine, a good contemporary authority, tells us that in 429 he sent St. Germanus,
Bishop of Auxerre, as his own representative (*vice sua*), to
uproot the evil.[5] The circumstances of the visit as related by
Germanus's biographer Constantius are pure fantasy, but the
actual journey of Germanus is entirely credible.[6] Pelagius was
a Briton, and a number of interesting letters, Pelagian in tone,
but probably written on the Continent,[7] confirm the impression
of Britain as active in intellectual and religious questions, and
as still in full rapport with Continental thought.[8]

Although Saxon raids must have rendered communications
with the Continent difficult and dangerous, they certainly did
not prevent them, as the colonisation of Brittany makes clear;
as does also the evidence of the inscriptions on the west coast of
Britain, and of voyages such as that of St Columbanus and
his companions.[9] Even more than Saxon pirates, the barbarian
invasions of Gaul and the consequent disorganisation of the

country must have sadly hampered regular contact between the British Church and Rome. The British Church inevitably failed to keep in touch with every new development of the Continental Church, and involuntarily became to a considerable extent self-dependent, while Continental interest in Britain must have lessened as the troubles in Gaul increased. Thus, naturally Continental information about the British Church ceases with the fifth century. Henceforth our information is derived from native sources.

Traditions are consistent in their echoes of the westward spread of Christianity beyond the borders of the Roman Empire at this period. In the fifth century the northern half of Ireland was converted by St Patrick[10]—a native of western Britain, probably of Strathclyde or the Solway area. The south of Ireland probably became Christian earlier. Wales had probably —but again not certainly—been Christian from Roman times. An eighth-century tradition claims that the earliest missionary in North Britain was St Ninian. Bede (*H.E.* III, 4) records a tradition, apparently from an oral source (*'ut perhibent'*), that 'long before' the conversion of the Northern Picts by St Columba the Southern Picts had accepted the true faith from the preaching of Ninian,[11] who had been trained correctly[12] (*edoctus regulariter*) in it and its mysteries at Rome. Bede adds that the church containing his tomb was named after St Martin—though he does not actually state that this was already its dedication in Ninian's day—and that his own episcopal seat was 'now' in the possession of the English. Finally he tells us that his *locus* was known as *Candida Casa* ('the White House'),[13] 'because he there built a church of stone which was unusual among the British'. We already know from the early inscribed stones that an important Christian community had been established at Whithorn in Roman times, and that it had survived the Northumbrian conquest with no apparent break

till the revival of the old bishopric, or the establishment of a
new one early in the eighth century. About this time a *Life* of
St Ninian was composed, which we no longer possess, and
shortly afterwards two poems, still extant;[14] but the twelfth-
century life by St Ailred of Rievaulx has very little independent
value.[15]

The earliest Welsh saint[16] of the native tradition is Dubricius
(Welsh *Dyfrig*), whose churches are on the River Wye but
whose *Life* is not earlier than the twelfth century. His most
distinguished pupil was St Illtud, who became the first abbot
of the monastery of Llantwit Major, and whose traditional
reputation for high intellectual prestige receives support from
the number of inscribed crosses still preserved on the spot, and
from the *Lives* of his contemporaries. The earliest *Life* of a
Welsh saint, that of St Samson,[17] possibly written in the seventh
century, claims that Samson was educated at Llantwit under
Illtud. The Breton Church was intellectually ahead of the
Welsh Church between the sixth and the ninth century, and
Samson was its greatest saint, thus confirming the intellectual
tradition of Llantwit.

Our earliest information of the Cornish Church shows it
as partaking of the monastic character of the Celtic Church
elsewhere, and medieval tradition claims that it was closely
dependent on that of Wales from the earliest times, when a
saintly 'family' of founders, 'children' of the eponymous king
of Brycheiniog, established Cornish monasticism.[18] The
similarity of the sculptured crosses of the two countries
indicates an early connection, and indeed the stone sculptures
are our earliest reliable evidence for the establishment of
Christianity in all the Celtic countries of the West. We have
no early records of the conversion of the Isle of Man, but here
again Christian sculpture has survived from the ninth century.
That the island was converted from the early Christian centre
of Whithorn, actually within sight, is highly probable, but the

most characteristic remains of Manx Christianity, the small Plate 63
rectangular churches or oratories known as *keeills*, have their
nearest affinities in Orkney. The remains of over 200 have been Plate 64
identified on the Isle of Man, a number in Christian church-
yards. That of Maughold contains four.

The sixth century is known in the history of the Celtic
Church as the 'Age of the Saints'. At this period the word
'saint' (*sanctus*) simply denotes any educated man, or a cleric,
a Christian trained in a monastic institution. It is the rapid
increase of these *sancti*, these educated 'religious', that has given
its name to the period. The Age of the Saints is, in fact, the
expression of a great wave of religious enthusiasm which
organised itself in the rise of monasticism.

This religious movement began during the late Roman
period in the Egyptian desert, where a number of ascetic
Christians instituted various forms of strict religious discipline,
some living in communities under a formulated 'rule', others
as solitaries in caves and cells over a wide area of the desert.
The movement spread from Egypt not only to Palestine,
Syria, and Mesopotamia, but also to lands farther west where
at this time the desire for solitude led to the foundation of
sanctuaries and cells on islands all round the coasts of western
Italy, to southern Gaul and western Spain, continuing along
the Breton coasts. Some of them attained high intellectual
importance. The island group of the Lérins, off the coast of
Cannes, founded *c.* 410 by St Honoratus, became a 'nursery
of bishops', and virtually a little university.[19]

In Britain, almost all the islands round the coast have tradi- Plates 56, 57
tions of the saints of this period. The most important is Iona,
founded by St Columba, and like Lérins a centre of study;
but the most impressive is Sceilg Mhichíl (Skellig Michael), a Plates 59, 60
bare and precipitous rock eight miles out in the Atlantic off
the coast of Co. Kerry, where the beehive-shaped cells, the

K

Plate 58

Plate 61

Plate 62

chapel, and the tiny graveyard of the monks still stand.[20] Equally ascetic in their solitude are Inishmurray, 4 miles off the Sligo coast; and in Scotland North Rona, nearly 60 miles north of the Butt of Lewis, and Sula Sgeir to the north-west.[21] Bardsey Island off the tip of the Caernarvonshire Peninsula is claimed as 'the burial-place of 20,000 saints',[22] and Lindisfarne (Holy Island), Caldy Island in South Wales, and Ynys Seiriol off Anglesey, are among scores of others which could be named. In Orkney the Brough of Deerness east of Kirkwall and the Brough of Birsay[23] on the west, are both tidal, as is Nendrum in Strangford Lough in Ireland. Lismore in Loch Linnhe at the mouth of the Great Glen developed into a medieval bishopric. All of these, as well as the island of Burra in Shetland, and Glastonbury and Tintagel in the southern part of Britain, probably contained sizeable communities, though often the recluse monks themselves lived apart, somewhat retired from the communities to which they were probably technically attached. In such cases they commonly lived in pairs for mutual confession.

Many of our own place-names retain echoes of their ascetic life. For example, *Merthyr* was once a *martyrium*, an anchorite retreat, not necessarily the scene of a martyrdom. *Dysart* in Fife was once a *deserta*, the abode of a religious anchorite or of a community. Indeed this word came to be synonymous with the monastic community of the early Celtic Church.

Side by side with the development of the anchorite retreats was the rise and spread of monasticism. An outstanding personality of religious force would inevitably attract followers who formed a community devoted to his ideals, and vowed to obey his precepts. Thus his austere life would become crystallised into a monastic 'rule'. Simultaneously his monastic retreat—his *deserta, uaimh, spelunca* or *martyrium*—would develop into a nucleated community, pledged to carry out the ideals of the saintly founder. The life of St Martin of Tours illustrates the process, starting with his original simple community in the cave cells of Ligugé, followed by his larger and more formal monastery, Marmoutier (*magnum monasterium*), and finally the establishment at Tours. In the same way Irish monasticism ascribed its beginning to St Finian, founder of Clonard; Welsh, to St Dyfrig of Henllan ('the Old Monastery') on the Wye; Breton, to St Samson of Dol; Gaelic Scotland, to St Columba of Iona; Strathclyde and Cumbria, to St Kentigern, with his earliest church at Hoddom in Dumfriesshire, his later at Glasgow, his traditional early nurture by St Serf in the 'cave' of Culross in Fife. By a reverse process a monastery would found a solitary retreat at a convenient distance, to which the religious could retire for periods of silence. Thus St Fructuosus of the Celtic Church in Spain early in the seventh century founded island monastic retreats off both the Galician coast and on the island of Cadiz in Baetica. Bede (*H. E.* II, 2) speaks of an anchorite as an habitual occupant of the monastery of Bangor (North Wales).

Plate 65

The anchorites of the stricter discipline are described in a later document, 'The Catalogue of the Saints of Ireland', as 'living in desert places' (*in locis desertis*), and as subsisting on herbs and water and alms, and possessing nothing of their own;[24] but the monastic ideals of the period everywhere placed purity of heart and simplicity of life even above formal observances, and Bede has unstinted praise for their sanctity. There was no flaw in their doctrine. They were perfectly orthodox, and they clung devotedly to the faith and precepts which they had received from their *seniores*. But two serious disadvantages militated against their survival, and both were the result of the circumstances of their earlier history. The first was the absence of central organisation. Each monastery with its dependencies was a self-governing unit, with its own rules and its own order of Mass. The second was that, owing to its remote position and the serious difficulties of communication,

Britain had failed to keep pace with changes that had periodically taken place in the Continental Church, and so was in certain respects out of complete conformity of usage.

In the Age of the Saints this lack of unity and complete conformity was not serious. There was no clash. Indeed, the greatest development of the Celtic Church took place at this time under St Columba from the island of Iona in Scotland, and still later under his successors in Northumbria. For over a thousand years the name of Columba has been revered as that of the greatest saint of the Celtic Church, and the founder of our most illustrious island sanctuary. The broad outline of his life is well known as it has come to us from his biographer Adamnán,[25] a descendant of Columba's grandfather, and later himself abbot of Iona; and though the *Life*, like all hagiography of that time, contains much that is inadmissible, yet in its broad outline it is a relatively trustworthy work. The picture of the saint which it presents is typical of the Celtic Church at its best, especially in his humility, his sanctity, and the simplicity of the life which he led.

Columba's traditional birthplace was Gartán in Donegal, and he was the great-grandson of Conall Gulbán, son of the founder of the Northern Uí Néill, the so-called High-King of Ireland. He himself stood near in the succession to the throne of Tara; but he abandoned his secular prospects, and *c.* 563 sailed to the newly founded kingdom of Dálriada in Scotland, and founded the monastery on Iona. From here, as we are told by Bede (*H. E.* III, 4) he converted the Northern Picts, at this time ruled by Brude mac Maelchon, whom Adamnán tells us the saint visited in his *villa regia*—possibly on more than one occasion—and whose *magus* ('wise man', also called his *nutricius*) he confounded by his miracles.

Many legends relate the cause of Columba's migration to Iona, none of them wholly satisfactory; but the kingdom of Dálriada, already probably Christian, must have offered scope for the statesmanship of this exceptionally able Christian priest. Subsequent history, as we learn from Adamnán, makes it clear that he was the strongest force in the new kingdom, and that he advised and directed its king Aedán mac Gabráin, and enjoyed his confidence throughout his life. His political relations with Brude must have been the paramount influence in securing the stability of both Dálriada, and the community of Iona. Everything that we know of him suggests that he was the most influential man in the political, no less than the spiritual, life of western Scotland in the sixth century.

Columba never became a bishop, and Bede notes it as a peculiarity of this branch of the Celtic Church that it was always ruled by presbyters. It is hardly less remarkable that, whereas few foundations are ascribed to his personal efforts, the abbot of Iona became the head of the largest and most powerful organisation of the Celtic Church. Moreover, though he is not represented as undertaking extensive missionary work, the Church of Iona rapidly spread throughout Scotland, and despite Bede's statement that the Southern Picts had been converted by St Ninian, it was the Columban Church which Nechtan IV dismissed across Druim Alban when he adopted the Roman rite in 717. Already in the early seventh century the monastery of Old Melrose had been founded in the tradition of Irish monasticism, and Eata, its first abbot, had been one of the twelve original pupils of St Aidan from Iona. St Cuthbert entered as a monk in 651 and from there visited the double monastery of Coldingham on St Abb's Head.

Plate 66

Plate 67

By a dramatic coincidence the date of the death of St Columba, A.D. 597, is also that of the arrival of St Augustine in Britain, coming as missionary from Rome to the Saxon kingdom in Kent. We are at the parting of the ways. The Celtic Church had many years of valuable spiritual life before it, and perhaps its greatest achievement, the establishment of

Christianity in Northumbria, was still in the future. Nevertheless the arrival of the great Augustine from Rome, and his establishment of the cathedral at Canterbury, constituted the beginning of the Church that was finally to supersede the Celtic Order, first in the Saxon kingdoms, and later throughout the British Isles.

The newly established Canterbury Church had two obvious duties before it—first to establish unity with the Christian British Church already established, and then to convert the Saxon kingdoms which still remained heathen. Bede relates how Augustine in the early days of his mission made two journeys to the western Border to seek to induce the British bishops and their most learned men (*plures viri doctissimi*) to observe Catholic unity and to join with him in preaching the Gospel to the heathen. Bede, our only authority for these meetings, tells the story in full saga style—the interviews, the scenes, the conversations, and the final conclusion and punishment of the obdurate British in the disastrous Battle of Chester in fulfilment of Augustine's prophecy. The whole is an admirably constructed short story, totally different in style from that in which the scriptorium at Canterbury would couch its documents. Perhaps Bede's informant was a Mercian monk, like Pecthelm, pupil of Aldhelm of Malmesbury, from whom he obtained other Mercian stories (*H.E.* V, 13, 18).

The next mission from Canterbury was directed towards the heathen of Northumbria. Bede tells us (*H.E.* I, 29) that Paulinus, who had accompanied Augustine from Pope Gregory, was sent north from Canterbury to the court of King Edwin as chaplain to his wife, and for long he sought the conversion of Edwin himself, till at last in 627 the king convened his counsellors at Whitby to ascertain their views. The story is too well known to need repeating here. We all recall the passage which first charmed us in Anglo-Saxon history—

the worldly and naïve speech of the heathen priest Coifi, and the moving idealism in the speech of the unnamed alderman who likened our brief span of life to that of the flight of a sparrow from the darkness of a stormy night through the brightness of a king's hall, then out into the darkness again: 'So is this life of man. Of what went before, or what will follow, we know nothing. If this new doctrine has something more certain we ought to follow it' (*H.E.* II, 13). This is where rhetoric and eloquence are indistinguishable.

The king was baptised at York in the same year. His subjects accepted the faith and for six years Paulinus continued to preach and baptise in Northumbria. His see was fixed at York, and the building of a splendid church there was begun; but before it could be completed Edwin perished in battle in 632 or 633, and a heathen reaction set in. Paulinus had to flee to Canterbury, taking the queen and her sons with him. A year later, with the restoration of the old royal line, Christianity was again restored by the new king Oswald (634–641), who during Edwin's reign had been living in exile in Scotland, and had received Christianity from the monks of Iona (Bede, *H.E.* III, 1).

The Christianity now introduced into Northumbria was very different in form from that of Paulinus earlier. Oswald appealed to Iona for help, and in response Aidan and a small group of monks established a monastery on the island of Lindisfarne, and within twenty years the Celtic form of Christianity was firmly established throughout Northumbria, with a rapid growth of monasticism, and the asceticism of Celtic practice. Bede, despite his whole-hearted devotion to the Roman Order, nevertheless bestows on the simplicity and beauty of Aidan's life the noblest praise accorded to anyone in his *Ecclesiastical History*.

The Celtic Church of Northumbria established by Aidan and his followers was in itself something of a mission Church, and in the following half-century Celtic missionaries had penetrated into many other parts of England, not only as independent ascetics but also as colleagues of Anglo-Saxon bishops and under the auspices of Anglo-Saxon kings. About the time of the withdrawal of Paulinus from Northumbria, East Anglia received a mission from Bishop Felix, who had been consecrated in Gaul; he was granted a see at Dunwich by the East Anglian king Sigeberht. Yet within a few years the king also allowed an Irish ascetic named Fursa to settle within his territory in a deserted fortress, probably Burgh Castle, and here he was succeeded by his brother Foilán.

Under Aidan's successor, Fínán, the Celtic form of Northumbrian Christianity was extended south of the Humber, and Peada, the son of the heathen king Penda, was baptised. Penda himself allowed four priests to settle in his territory, all of whom appear to have followed Irish usage, owing both origin and obedience to Lindisfarne; and the see of Mercia seems to have been independent of Canterbury till 699, when Archbishop Theodore fixed the seat at Lichfield. The position of the growth of Christianity in England has been justly summed up by Sir Frank Stenton: 'There is little profit in trying to assess the relative importance of the Irish and the Continental influences in the Conversion of the English. . . . The strands of Irish and Continental influence were interwoven in every kingdom, and at every stage of the process by which England became Christian.'[26]

There was no clash of doctrine or of ideals between the Celtic and the Roman Orders, no difference in the form or the functions of the hierarchy, or in the fundamental order of church services. The bishop was always and everywhere the spiritual head of the Church, and he alone had the right to consecrate other bishops, and all new churches and cemeteries. The rights of an abbot did not extend beyond the organisation of his monastery and its affiliations. These had, however, grown to be institutions of great power, as in Gaul, where their influence in episcopal elections was viewed with disfavour by Pope Celestine.[27] In England also a division arose which focused itself on differences of organisation. In details of procedure the Celtic Order seemed impracticably out-of-date to the Roman representatives at Canterbury. The most obvious of these discrepancies was the unreformed calculation of the date of Easter, resulting in not only a lack of uniformity in Church usage, but also in actual practical difficulties.

Already in the early seventh century a series of letters from Canterbury and Rome had urged the Irish and the Britons to conform with the rite of the Catholic Church and the peace and unity which it had spread throughout the world. In 629 most of the south of Ireland celebrated Easter according to the Roman dating, but it was nearly 60 years before the north of Ireland was finally brought to change its ancient usage. The reform was ultimately brought about largely through the efforts of the Northumbrian monk Ecgberht and Adamnán, abbot of Iona, who had been converted to the Roman usage during a visit to the Northumbrian court. It was not, however, until 716 that the Columban Church of Iona came under the Roman obedience, just about the time when Nechtan IV had accepted it for the Southern Picts. In Northumbria the change crystallised as a practical issue. The habits of King Oswiu, who had been trained in exile in Iona, were naturally those of the Celtic party, but his wife, a daughter of King Edwin, had been trained at Canterbury. Bede, with his natural instinct for a dramatic situation, pictures the court and the king celebrating Easter according to the old dating of the Celtic Church while the queen and her followers were still fasting and observing Palm Sunday. Obviously this could not continue, and at a 'synod' at Whitby in 663, the point was debated,[28] as a result of which the king gave his decision in favour of conformity to Roman usage.

There was no looking back. The Synod of Whitby inaugurated a new era for the Church in Britain, and the Roman obedience gradually spread throughout the Western World. Oswiu's son Ecgfrith (670–685), a zealous Christian, did much to develop the newly established uniformity. It was about this time that the Church spread northwards into the Scottish Lowlands. But important as the Synod of Whitby was in the history of the British Church it was only a detail in the widespread movement towards uniformity in the Church of western Europe. The monastic Church, established probably in the sixth century in Spanish Galicia, had already accepted the Easter reckoning and the Roman tonsure at the fourth Council of Toledo in 633,[29] and by the middle of the eighth century the change had become general in most of the Celtic foundations of central Europe. The end of the Celtic Church was in sight; but custom changes slowly, and the process was everywhere a gradual one. In Britain it was more than half a century after the Whitby Synod that the Southern Picts conformed, and in Wales not till after Bede's death. Our earliest notice for Wales is in the *Annales Cambriae* for 665, where it is stated that 'Easter is changed among the Britons'. In Devon and Cornwall, Bede tells us (*H.E.* V, 18), Aldhelm, abbot of Malmesbury and afterwards bishop of Sherborne, persuaded many of the Britons to conform,[30] but it was not till Athelstan's reign that the British bishop Conan submitted to Archbishop Wulfstan of Canterbury, and was nominated to the see of Bodmin in 936.

The controversy had not been inspired by petty issues. The timing of Easter and the nature of the tonsure were symbols of the fundamental principles for which the Celtic and the Roman parties were contending. British Christianity had had a long history and high ideals, and it was natural that the Celtic peoples should cling loyally to the traditional form with which they were familiar. On the other hand it was equally natural that those who had received their training from the cultured Continental centres should realise the paramount need for unity and obedience if Christianity was to survive. The issue was deeply serious and devoid of rancour, and the controversy was carried on with dignity and mutual respect. Perhaps the most remarkable feature of the long struggle is the absence of persecution. It would be idle to claim that political issues were not involved; but there is no record that either side made use of force. They were honourable opponents.

Looking back at this distance at time, we can realise something of the mental stimulus that the contest must have given to both the Celtic and the Roman parties. The absence of persecution was an all-important element in this stimulus, affording freedom for frank expression. Scriptoria were set a-buzzing to record whatever was deemed relevant to the claims of both parties. To the Celtic peoples especially it was important to set down in written form what had previously been transmitted orally and had been good enough for home use, but stood no chance beside the cultured written documents of the Roman party. The *Lives* of the Celtic saints must be recorded, and the basic traditions of their 'rule'. We may probably attribute the rise and spread of written literature among the Celtic peoples largely to the need felt to record their traditions and their customs in a manner worthy to compete with their more cultured opponents. Indeed, we may go further and claim that most of the literature of our period in Britain—Celtic and Saxon alike—was inspired directly or indirectly by the need felt by them to articulate the ideals for which they were contending, and which resulted in the greatest intellectual movement in the first millennium of our history. Bede's contribution to the history of the Church in Britain, and to our own early history, was prompted by his desire to offer a worthy picture of the Roman Church, to the service of which he had given his life, and which he lived to see supreme in our Islands.

Notes to Chapters

Chapter I

1 Jackson, *P.B.A.*
2 Jackson in Wainwright, *P.P.*, Appendix.
3 D. F. Allen, F.S.A., 'The Origins of Coinage in Britain: A Reappraisal' in *Problems of the Iron Age in Southern Britain*, edited by S. S. Frere, published as Occasional Paper II (1960) *U.L.I.A.*
4 Richmond, *R.B.*, 155.
5 *Ibid.*, *R.N.*, 113.
6 Atkinson, *C.B.*, 7.
7 White, *L.S.*, *passim*.
8 *Panégyriques Latins*, ed. Galletier, Vol. I, 122.
9 *Ibid.*, 91.
10 *Epistola VIII*, vi.
11 Ammianus Marcellinus, *Rerum Gestarum Libri* XXVII, viii, 1.
12 See Charlesworth, *L.P.*, 26; Collingwood and Myres, 287.
13 The identification was made by Stevens, *É.C.* III (1938) 86.
14 *Poems of Claudian*, Panegyric on Stilicho's Consulship II, 247.
15 *Ibid.*, *In Eutropium* I, 392.
16 *Vandal War* III, ii.
17 *Historia* V, v, vi, x, Zosimus derived his information about events in Britain from a Byzantine historian, Olympiodorus, who dealt mainly with western events. He was an exact contemporary of the last days of the Roman Occupation of Britain, and is of a high degree of authenticity. See also Thompson, *Antiquity* XXX (1956), 163–7.
18 Eutropius IX, XXI.
19 For the preceding suggestions relating to these late officials I am indebted to the invaluable article by Stevens on the *Notitia Dignitatum* (cf. p. 167 below).
20 Zosimus, *Historia* VI, v, 3 and 10.
21 *L.P.*, 34.
22 See references cited by Chadwick, *S.E.B.H.*, 11, note; and cf. more recently Richmond, *R.B.*, 185.

CHAPTER II

1 Wheeler, *Lydney.*
2 As Professor Richmond reminds us *R.B.*, 64, 140.
3 Richmond, *R.B.*, 192.
4 Frere, *A.J.* XL (1960), 20.
5 Caspari, *Briefe*, 15.
6 See Dio Cassius, LV, xxiii; and cf. Collingwood and Myres, 172; Rivet, *T.C.R.B.*, 136.
7 Nash-Williams, *E.C.I.W.*, p. 14.
8 Jackson, *Antiquity* XXIX (1955); cf. H. M. Chadwick, *E.S.*, ch. X; cf. also Hunter Blair, *O.N.*, 36.
9 I have discussed this term in *B.B.C.S.* XIX (1961), 225
10 Jackson, *loc. cit.*
11 See the study of the Votadini by Hogg in Grimes, *A.A.B.*, 100.
12 The scarlet tunic was one of the insignia of Roman military officers, including those of the federate states.
13 For their early history see O'Rahilly, *E.I.H.M.*, 64; Jackson, *L.H.E.B.*, 155. Two versions of the Irish saga are extant, both dating from the eighth century, and both contained in manuscripts in the Bodleian Library at Oxford. The version contained in the Oxford MS. known as Rawlinson B 502 has been edited and translated into English by the late Kuno Meyer in *Y. Cymmrodor* XIII (1900), and later in *Ériu* III (1907), 135. See more recently Spender, in *Essays and Studies presented to Professor Tadg ua Donnchada (Féilscribhinn Torna* (Cork, 1947), 211).
14 For a discussion of the possible relationship between the terms *gwledic* and *protector*, see E. K. Chambers, *Arthur of Britain* (London, 1927), 176; cf. Stevens, *É.C.* III (1938), 86 ff.; and my note in *B.B.C.S.* XXIX (1961), 225.
15 The chief early references are cited in a recent study of Vortigern by Radford, *Antiquity* XXXII (1958), 19; cf. further H. M. Chadwick, *The Origin of the English Nation* (Cambridge, 1907), 37, and later *ibid.*, *S.E.B.H.*, 21.
16 Nash-Williams, *E.C.I.W.*, no. 182, Plates XXXV, XXXVI.
17 Bu'lock, *Antiquity* XXXIV (1960), 49.
18 The name has been associated by antiquarian speculation or tradition with Dinas Emrys ('the citadel of Ambrosius'), in Snowdonia, at

least from the twelfth century. Dr Savory's recent excavations have proved that the site was occupied in the late Roman and sub-Roman periods, probably in the late fourth and fifth centuries A.D. and again in the sixth to eighth centuries A.D. See his important article, in *A.C.* IX (1960), 13.

19 Jackson, 'The Arthur of History', and 'Arthur in Early Welsh Verse', in R. S. Loomis, *A.L.*, 1, 12; also Thomas Jones, *B.B.C.S.* XVII (1960), 235.

20 See Crawford, *Antiquity* IX (1935), 289; Jackson, *M.P.* XLIII (1945). Count Nikolai Tolstoy, in *B.B.C.S.* XIX (1961), 118.

21 For valuable notes on the literary evidence relating to Arthur, see Bromwich, *Triads*, 358, 521.

22 Collingwood and Myres, *R.B.E.S.*; Clarke, *E.A.*, 129; Dauncey, *Antiquity* XVI (1942); Myres, *ibid.*, and in Harden, *D.A.B.*, 37; for a full recent summary, Myres, *C.B.A.*, Report no. 11 (1961), 40. Cf. Richmond, *R.B.*, 65; for coins, see Sutherland, in Harden, *D.A.B.*, 3; Allen, in Frere, *U.L.I.A.*

23 For a study of the *curach*, see Marcus, *S.G.S.* VII (1953), 106.

24 C. O'Rahilly, *I.W.*, ch. 2; Wheeler, *P.R.W.*, 234, 292; Stevens, *Mélanges* XLII, 671.

25 See Wrenn, *T.H.S.C.* (1959), 38; Melville Richards, *J.R.S.A.I.* XC (1960), 145.

26 J. Loth, *L'Émigration.*

27 Full references are given by the present writer in *The Age of the Saints in the Early Celtic Church* (Oxford, 1961), 58.

CHAPTER III

1 See Jackson, 'The Pictish Language', ch. VI in Wainwright, *P.P.*

2 Reference may be made to a paper by the present writer: 'The name Pict', *S.G.S.* VIII (1958).

3 The name is basically identical with that of Maelgwn, the ruler of North Wales (cf. p. 70 below).

4 Is this Bede's translation of a Celtic title comparable to the Irish *árd-rí* ('high-king'), and the British *Ver-tigernas* ('chief lord'), later *Vortigern*?

5 Jackson, 'The Pictish Language', in Wainwright, *P.P.*, 139.

6 Reference may be made among other examples to a suspicious document claiming to be an ancient record of the foundation of St Andrews, which claims that the scribe has copied the contents as they are found in *veteribus Pictorum libris.* See H. M. Chadwick, *E.S.*, 28. Cf. M. O. Anderson, *S.H.R.* XXIX (1950), 17. Cf. also p. 56 above.

7 Most of the texts of the early Chronicles were published by Skene, *P.S.*, and discussed by him in *C.S.* I. For detailed extracts, translated into English, see A. O. Anderson, *E.S.* I, *passim*, and cf. especially the Bibliographical Notes, xiv. For a general study of the subject see H. M. Chadwick, *E.S.*, *passim.* An indispensable study is that of M. O. Anderson in three contributions to *S.H.R.* XXVIII, 1 and 2 (1949), XXIX (1950). The best version of the Pictish king lists is that of Skene, *P.S.*, 4.

8 Cf. H. M. Chadwick, *E.S.*, 81.

9 See H. M. Chadwick, *E.S.*, 96, 98, and important references there cited. Nearly all the king lists are printed in full in Skene, *P.S.*

10 For a general outline reference may be made to H. M. Chadwick, *E.S.*, 121, though this study now needs to be checked by the later researches of M. O. Anderson, especially as indicated in the references to the *S.H.R.* (see above).

11 On this subject see M. O. Anderson, *S.H.R.* XXIX (1950), 18.

12 On the Scottish king-lists see M. O. Anderson, *S.H.R.* XXVIII (1949), 108.

13 In the Irish language *Eirc* is the genitive of *Erc*; *Gabráin* of *Gabrán*, etc.

14 Notably the Synchronisms by Flann Mainistrech and the *Duan Albanach* by an unknown author. The fullest edition of this poem is by Jackson, *Celtica* III (1955), 149. The most useful work is the text, translation and commentary by the same scholar in *S.H.R.* XXXVI (1959), 125.

15 Published by Skene, *P.S.*, 308.

16 See the important note by O'Rahilly, *E.I.H.M.*, 371, and n. 1.

17 Text A. See Skene, *P.S.*, 8.

18 See Jackson, 'The Britons of Southern Scotland', *Antiquity* XXIX (1955), 77; D. Kirby, *T.C.W.S.* LXII (n.s. 1962).

19 See Jackson, *loc. cit.*; and more fully by the same author 'The Northern British Section in Nennius', in *C.S.*, edited by the present writer.

20 See Bromwich, 'The Welsh Tradition', *S.E.B.H.*, 83.

21 See 'Early Culture and Learning in North Wales', by the present writer, *S.E.B.C.*, 1.

22 Skene, *F.A.B.W.* I, 65, 66.

23 Bromwich, *Triads*, no. 84.

CHAPTER IV

1 The best text is that of Sir Ifor Williams, *Armes Prydein* (Cardiff, 1955). An early and less satisfactory text and translation are given under the name of Skene, *F.A.B.W.* I, 436; II, 123.

2 According to Lloyd (*H.W.* I, 256, n. 155) it was used in later times in a restricted sense, exclusive of Gwent and Morgannwg. See also the note in Stevenson's edition of Asser's *Life of King Alfred*, 233–4.

3 A district between the Wye and the Severn.

4 The translation is that of Lloyd-Jones. See 'The Court Poets of the Welsh Princes', *P.B.A.* XXXIV (1948), 23.

5 See Jackson, 'The Britons in southern Scotland', *Antiquity* XXIX (1955), 77.

6 *Meriaun filius eius divisit possessiones inter fratres suos.*

7 Lloyd, (*H.W.* I, 118), following Zimmer, regards this statement as an arbitrary treatment of the source, and not in itself likely to be correct.

8 See the pedigrees edited by Wade-Evans, *V.S.*, 315, and cf. the *Life of St Cadoc*, edited and translated *ibid.*, ch. 46.

9 The precise position of the palace of Aberffraw has not been identified. For some recent notes on the subject see Hague, 'Some Light on the Site of the Palace of Aberffraw', and also Professor Glanville R. J. Jones, 'The Site of Llys Aberffraw', both in the *T.A.A.S.*, 1957.

10 For the text and commentary of the letter see Derolez, *L'Antiquité Classique* XXI (1952), no. 2, 359; *ibid.*, *Runica Manuscripta* (Bruges, 1954), 97. For further references and details see N. K. Chadwick, *S.E.B.C.*, 94.

11 On this subject see Lloyd, *H.W.* I, 324.

12 I. Williams, *W.P.*, 48.

13 For references and some discussion of this identification, see N. K. Chadwick, *S.E.B.C.*, 75.

14 See the genealogical table in Lloyd, *H.W.* II, 765.

15 See the list of these charters and attestations in Lloyd, *H.W.* I, 353.

16 Brooke, *English Coins from the Seventh Century to the Present Day* (3rd ed., London, 1950), 57, 60; Pl. XV, 1. Mr Michael Dolley has pointed out to me that the coins of Gillys, of Eadred, Eadwig, and Eadgar which do not have a mint signature are of a style which can be associated with the immediate vicinity of Chester, and the coin of Hywel is of this style also.

CHAPTER V

1 See Thurneysen, *S.E.I.L.*, *passim*.

2 Binchy, *Ériu* XII.

3 For the text of the Welsh Laws, see the List of Primary Authorities below.

4 Binchy, *L.L.A.*, 175, 23, 17; further *Celtica* III (1935).

5 For a brief study of the subject see my article on 'Pictish and Celtic Marriage in Early Literature and Tradition', *S.G.S.* VIII (1955).

6 See Fraser, 'The Alleged Matriarchy of the Picts', in *Medieval Studies in Memory of Gertrude Schopperle Loomis* (1927).

7 For the *Cymru* claiming to be of pure blood, see Seebohm, *T.S.W.*, 61.

8 *Description of Wales* I, 17.

9 See Ellis, *W.T.L.*, 46.

10 Binchy, *L.L.A.*

11 Seebohm, *T.C.A.L.*, 298.

12 *Ibid.*, 306.

13 *Ibid.*, 307.

14 Jackson, *Antiquity* XXIX (1955), 88.

15 Ellis, I, 212.

16 Edwards, *P.B.A.* LXII (1956), 158.

17 Lloyd, *H.W.* I, 301.

18 For the questions of the authenticity, date and authorship, see Edwards, *H.D.W.L.*—an invaluable study.

19 See the Life of St John the Almoner included in *Three Byzantine Saints*, translated from the Greek by Dawes and Baynes (Oxford, 1948), ch. 10, 217.

20 Alcock, *B.B.C.S.* XVI (1954), 242.

21 Aileen Fox, *A.J.* XXXV (1955), 55.

22 Thomas, *Proceedings of the West Cornwall Field Club,* Vol. II (1956–7); *ibid., M.A.* III (1959). Radford in Harden, *D.A.B.*, 59.

23 Williams, *Canu Aneirin*, line 1101; Introduction, 50; Translation, *T.A.A.S.*, 1935.

24 Savory, *D.H.S.* LXXI (1958), 166.

25 Hogg, *Arch. J.* CXVII (1960), 1.

26 Savory, *A.J.* CIX (1961), 13.

27 See Feacham's important study in Wainwright, *P.P.*, ch. III.

28 Craw, *P.S.A.S.* LXIV (1930), 126; Piggott, *ibid.,* LXXXVI, 193.

29 Alcock, *A.C.* CIX (1960), 78.

30 A number of earth-houses in Angus and Perthshire were excavated by the late F. T. Wainwright, and a comprehensive survey and study of the subject by him has recently been published: *The Souterrains of Southern Pictland* (London, 1963). A brief survey was published in *Antiquity* XXVII (1953), 219. The account by Joseph Anderson, *S.I.A.* I, 300 is still valuable and contains some good line drawings.

31 Clark, *Cornish Fogous* (London, 1961).

32 Richmond, *J.R.S.* LI (1961), 160.

33 Megaw, *P.I.M.* V (1950), 171. Part of perhaps the culvert here referred to has been found on the site.

34 A. O. Curle, *T.T.*, 108.

35 Brailsford, *M.T.*

36 ÓRíordáin, *P.R.I.A.*, Vol. LI, Section C, no. 3 (Dublin, 1947), 43.

37 O'Dell, *Antiquity* XXXIII (1959), 241; O'Dell and Cain, *St Ninian's Isle Treasure* (Aberdeen, 1960).

38 See the exhaustive recent study by Wilson and Blunt, *Archaeologia* XCVIII (1961), 75.

39 A complete list and a plate of these coins is given by Aileen Fox, *H.Y.W.A.*, 118, 121 and Plate IX.

40 *A.C.* LXXXIX (1934), 1.

41 Alcock, *B.B.C.S.* XVIII (1960), 221; Savory, in Harden, *D.A.B.*, 40.

42 Caves were probably the best type of private dwelling in the Dark Ages, and their owners well above the poverty line.

CHAPTER VI

1 Recent opinion tends to seek the origin of the ogam alphabet in the Latin grammar schools of the later Roman Empire, as represented by Donatus in the fourth century. See Jackson, *E.C.N.-W.E.*, 203.

2 *De Bello Gallico* VI, xiii.

3 See Binchy, *Ériu* XII, 41, 71.

4 See Du Cange, s.v. *nutritor*; and cf. Gregory of Tours, *Hist. Franc.* viii, 22.

5 Williams, *C.T.*, 1. Cf. further Bromwich, *Triads*, 319.

6 Edited by I. Williams, *C.A.* A valuable account of the poem and commentary on the above edition is published by Jackson, *Antiquity* XIII (1939), 25.

7 The translation is that of Bromwich, in Chadwick, *S.E.B.H.*, 88.

8 For a brief discussion of these poems, see Bromwich, *Triads*, 470; H. M. and N. K. Chadwick, *Growth* I, 106.

9 For parallels see 'Geilt', *S.G.S.* V. (1942), 106, by the present writer.

10 For some account of Sir Ifor Williams's views on the Llywarch Hen poems, see *E.W.P.*, 31; *P.B.A.*, 1932.

11 The *Cynddylan* Cycles of poems here quoted formed part of broadcast scripts by Glyn Jones, T. J. Morgan and I. Williams, the first two under the title of *The Saga of Llywarch the Old*; the third by Morgan, *The Misfortunes of Princess Heledd*. I am indebted to Professor Morgan for his kindness in giving me a copy of the third script and permission to quote it here; and to Sir Ifor Williams for similar permission to quote his translations both here and elsewhere.

12 Williams, *E.W.P.*, 59.

13 For a recent brief statement on this subject see Parry, *O.B.W.V.* (Introduction).

14 The title given by Lady Charlotte Guest to the collection of translations which she published in 1839. The MS. of the Red Book of Hergest uses the term *Mabinogi* for the first four stories.

15 *H.W.L.*, 87.

16 'Helen of the Hosts' figures in the Harleian Genealogy 2 as the ancestress of the Dyfed royal Dynasty. She has become confused with Helen, the mother of the Emperor Constantine.

17 Edited and translated by Whitley Stokes (London, 1872).

18 A brief survey of this subject has been made by the present writer in 'The Lost Literature of Celtic Scotland', *S.G.S.* VII (1953), 115.

19 Edited and translated by Wade-Evans, *V.S.* 24.

20 See the versions summarised by Thurneyson, *Die Irische Helden und Königsage* (Halle-am-Saale, 1921), 377.

21 These have been studied by the present writer in 'The Story of Macbeth', *S.G.S.* VI (1949), 189; VII (1951), 1.

22 Translations by R. Bromwich, *Triads*.

CHAPTER VII

1 J. Anderson, *R.A.*, iv.

2 See Jackson, *L.H.E.B.*, 120.

3 Nash-Williams, *E.C.M.W.*, 4. The numbers in the text below refer throughout to this book.

4 *Ibid.*, fig. 75; 2, 88.

5 *Ibid.*, no. 182; Pl. XXXV–XXXVI; 123.

6 Hencken, *A.C.S.*, 226.

7 Radford, *J.R.I.C.*, n.s. I, 117; Macalister, *C.I.I.C.*, I, no. 487.

8 Hencken, 272.

9 Langdon, 356.

10 *Ibid.*, 359.

11 Kinvig, 42.

12 Kermode, *M.C.*, Pl. XV: Allen, *Christian Symbolism*, p. 144. Megaw, *J.M.M.* VI (1958).

13 Talbot Rice, *E.A.*, 104.

14 J. Anderson, *S.E.C.T.* I, 247; Macalister, *S.I.I.C.* I, no. 510; Kermode, *Z.C.P.* I, 48 (and Plate).

15 J. Anderson, *S.E.C.T.* I, 251.

16 *P.A.*, 97.

17 *R.A.*, xi.

18 Stevenson, *P.A.*, 102, 103.

19 Henderson, *P.S.A.S.* XCI (1957–58).

20 C. Curle, *P.S.A.S.* LXXIV (1939–40).

21 Cruden, *E.C.P.M.S.*, Pl. 41.

22 Radford, *Antiquity* XVI (1942), 10.

23 Allen, *E.C.M.S.*, Aberlemno 3, no. XXXVI; fig. 228; 215.

24 As C. Mowbray (née Curle) emphasises, *Antiquity* X (1936).

CHAPTER VIII

1 For the earliest references to Christianity in Britain, see H. Williams, *C.E.B.*, 1–138; J. M. C. Toynbee, *J.B.A.A.* XVI (1953).

2 Levison, 'St Alban and St Albans', *Antiquity* XV (1941), 337.

3 Richmond, *Arch. J.* CIII (1947), 64.

4 For Pelagius, see de Plinval, *Pélage, ses Écrits, sa Vie, et sa Réforme* (Lausanne, 1943); Ferguson, *Pelagius* (Cambridge, 1956).

5 *Epitoma Chronicon*, at 429.

6 The present writer has discussed the evidence for St Germanus in *P.L.*, ch. 9.

7 Edited by Caspari, and translated by Haslehurst. For more precise references see the present writer in Chadwick, *S.E.B.H.*, 210.

8 The literary evidence has been collected by the writer in Chadwick, *ibid.*, ch. 8.

9 The precise details of his route are not recorded. For a general account see Kenney, *S.E.H.I.*, 187; Walker, *S.C.O.* IX.

10 For recent works on St Patrick, see the studies of Bury, Bieler and Carney. The most recent and authoritative is that of Binchy, *S.H.* 2 (1962), 1.

11 The most recent study of St Ninian is by MacQueen.

12 Or possibly 'according to monastic discipline'.

13 The name undoubtedly refers to the exceptional building technique of dressed stone, in contrast to the wooden buildings which were common at that period. Cf. Belgrade (*Beograd*, 'White City') or the popular name of Moscow in Russian folk-songs, *Belokamennaya Moskva*, 'Moscow of the white stone walls', referring to the dressed stone, faceted or rusticated, of the Kremlin.

14 For an account of these documents and their relationship to the Ninian tradition see Levison, *Antiquity* XIV (1940), 280.

15 I have discussed some aspects of St Ninian in *T.D.G.S.* XXVII (1959), 9.

16 Evidence relating to individual British saints is collected by Baring-Gould and Fisher, *L.B.S.* A recent comprehensive series of studies of the *Lives* of the saints of Cornwall, Brittany, and Wales by the late Canon Doble, published in 'The Cornish Saints' series over a number of years at various places in southern England and Wales is valuable. For the saints more especially of Wales, see also Bowen, *Settlements*; also Conway Davies, *J.H.S.C.W.*; for Cornwall, see Chope, Halliday, Hencken; for Somerset, see Radford, *P.S.A. Som.*; for the Isle of Man, see Ashley, Kinvig.

17 Chief text and study by Fawtier, Engl. transl. by Taylor.

18 Baring-Gould and Fisher, I, 318; Gougaud, *C.C.L.*, 102, n. 2; Chope, *B.H.*, ch. II, and Appendices, pp. 210, 212.

19 Cooper-Marsdin, *H.I.L.*, 54. For the island sanctuaries in western Europe see also N. K. Chadwick, *P.L.*, ch. VI.

20 See M. and L. de Paor, *E.C.I.*, 54.

21 J. Anderson, *S.E.C.T.* I, 113 ff.; Stewart, *Ronay* (Oxford, 1937); Nisbet and Gailey, *Arch. J.* CXVI (1961), 88.

22 Book of Llandav, 282.

23 Radford, *Birsay*; *ibid.*, in Wainwright, *N.I.*, 113, 160.

24 For the date and value of this document see Grosjean, *A.B.* LXXIII (1955), and for the text see Haddan and Stubbs, *Councils* II, Pt. II, 292.

25 Edited by Reeves, also more recently (with English translation) by A. O. and M. O. Anderson; and for Adamnán's sources, see the latter, p. 18, with important references to Brüning and to Kenney.

26 *Anglo-Saxon England²*, (Oxford, 1950), 124.

27 See his famous letter to the bishops in Gaul in 428, Mansi, *Councils* III, 264; Migne, *Patrologiae Latinae* I, col. 430.

28 Bede (*H.E.* III, 25), following a widespread literary convention, reports the debate in the style of a dispute between two opponents before a judge. See also the account by Eddius in his *Life of Bishop Wilfrid*, Colgrave, *Eddius*, Cap. X.

29 Haddan and Stubbs, *Councils* II, Pt. I, 99.

30 By his famous letter to King '*Geruntius* (Gereint) *Occidentalis regni*', i.e. Devon and Cornwall. Haddan and Stubbs, *Councils* III, 268.

Some Works of Reference and Sources

I CONTINENTAL

The Notitia Dignitatum ('Register of Officials'), fifth century, relates to the organisation of the late Roman Empire, comprising lists of officials, civil and military, and the troops and forts which they held. Ed. Otto Seeck (Berlin, 1876); see Stevens, *A.J.* XCVII (1940), 125; Birley, *T.C.W.S.*, XXXIX (1939), 190; White, *L.S.*

Two contemporary Latin Chronicles, the *Epitoma Chronicon* of Prosper of Aquitaine, and the *anonymous Gaulish Chronicle*. Ed. J. Mommsen, in *Mon. Germ. Hist.: Auct. Antiq.*, IX, *Chronica Minora* (Berlin, 1892).

Vegetius, *Epitoma Rei Militaris,* fourth century, an account of the Roman army. Ammianus Marcellinus, later fourth century; Zosimus, late fifth century; and Procopius mid-sixth century, all have incidental references specified in the text above.

Roman panegyrists and poets of Gaul from the third to the fifth century. See especially W. Baehrens *XII Panegyrici Latini* (Leipzig, 1911); E. Galletier, *Panégyrics Latins,* I (Paris, 1949), with French translation. See references also in the works of Ausonius (fourth century), Rutilius Namatianus (early fifth century), Claudian (late fourth and early fifth century), Sidonius Apollinaris (late fifth century).

The *Life of St Germanus*, ed. W. Levison in *Mon. Germ. Hist.: Script. Rer. Merov.* VII (Berlin, 1920), 225.

II BRITISH

Inscriptions on stone, from the fifth to the seventh century: Macalister, *C.I.I.C.*; Nash-Williams, *E.C.M.W.*

Gildas, *De Excidio Britanniae*: ed. and transl. by H. Williams (London, 1899). The text claims to be of the sixth century.

The *Historia Brittonum,* 'The History of the Britons', early ninth century: ed. F. Lot (French edition and translation, Paris, 1934); A. W. Wade-Evans, *Nennius's History of the Britons* (London, 1938), an English translation of the above, including also the *Annales Cambriae* and other matter from MS Brit. Mus., Harley 3859—a very useful and important compendium.

Genealogies of the Welsh princes, those from MS Harley 3859 (the South Welsh version) edited by Wade-Evans, as above; also by J. Loth, *Les Mabinogion,* II (Paris, 1913), 326. Those in MS XX, Jesus College, Oxford (the North Welsh version), ed. M. E. Phillimore, *Y Cymmrodor* VIII (1887), IX (1888). Twelve genealogies of the North British princes, contained in MS Hengwrt 536, are edited by Skene, *F.A.B.W.* II (Edinburgh, 1868), 454 Genealogies of the Welsh saints, mostly related to the princes, are edited by Wade-Evans, *V.S.B.G.,* 320.

The Welsh Laws, ed. and transl. by Wade-Evans, *W.M.L.*; English translation of the 'Dimetian Code' by Melville Richards, *L.H.D.* (See p. 180 for bibliographical references.)

Lives of British saints. The chief edition, with English translation, of the *Lives* of the Welsh saints is that of A. W. Wade-Evans, *V.S.B.G.*; cf. further Ch. IX, note 16 above. Adamnán's *Life of St Columba,* ed. Reeves; also ed. and transl. by A. O. and M. O. Anderson.

Early Welsh bardic poetry. These early poems were published with an English translation by Skene, in *F.A.B.W.* More scholarly and reliable texts have been published recently by Sir Ifor Williams. See the references in Ch. VI above.

Collections of verses composed for mnemonic purposes, such as the *Beddau* ('the Graves'), which lists the final resting-places of the great heroes of the past: ed. and transl. by Skene, *F.A.B.W.* I, p. 309; II, p. 28: now in process of being re-edited. A number of collections of a form of literature known as *Triads,* ed. and transl. by R. Bromwich, *Triads.*

A valuable incidental source is *Asser's Life of King Alfred,* ed. and transl. by W. H. Stevenson (Oxford, 1904, new impression, 1959); the *Historia Ecclesiastica,* by the Venerable Bede; ed. Charles Plummer

(Oxford, 1896); transl. John Stevenson (London, 1910); revised edition, 1954; also transl. L. Sherley-Price (Harmondsworth, 1955).

The Irish annals contain much of importance for Celtic Britain, especially the *Annals of Ulster,* ed. and transl. in 4 vols. by W. M. Hennessy (Dublin, 1887–1901); the *Annals of Tigernach,* ed. and partly transl. by Whitley Stokes, in *R.C.* XVI, XVII, XVIII; the *Annals of Inisfallen,* ed. and transl. Seán Mac Airt (Dublin, 1951).

Key to Selected Periodicals referred to in the Notes on the Text

GENERAL

A.B.	*Analecta Bollandiana*
A.C.	*Archaeologia Cambrensis*
A.J.	*The Antiquaries Journal*
ARCH. J.	*Archaeological Journal*
B.B.C.S.	*Bulletin of the Board of Celtic Studies*
C.B.A.	*Council for British Archaeology Reports*
D.H.S.	*Denbighshire Historical Society*
E.A.	*Episcopal Acts relating to Welsh Dioceses, 1066–1272*
É.C.	*Études Celtiques*
E.H.R.	*English Historical Review*
J.B.A.A.	*Journal of the British Archaeological Association*
J.H.S.C.W.	*Journal of the Historical Society of the Church in Wales*
J.M.M.	*Journal of the Manx Museum*
J.R.I.C.	*Journal of the Royal Institute of Cornwall,* Second Series
J.R.S.	*Journal of Roman Studies*
J.R.S.A.I.	*Journal of the Royal Society of Antiquaries of Ireland*
M.A.	*Medieval Archaeology*
M.P.	*Modern Philology*
P.B.A.	*Proceedings of the British Academy*
P.I.M.	*Proceedings of the Isle of Man Natural History and Antiquarian Society* (New series)
P.P.S.	*Proceedings of the Prehistoric Society*
P.R.I.A.	*Proceedings of the Royal Irish Academy*

P.S.A.S.	*Proceedings of the Society of Antiquaries of Scotland*
P.S.A. SOM.	*Proceedings of the Somersetshire Archaeological Society*
R.C.	*Revue celtique*
R.E.A.	*Revue des Études anciennes*
S.G.S.	*Scottish Gaelic Studies*
S.H.	*Studia Hibernica*
S.H.R.	*Scottish Historical Review*
T.A.A.S.	*Transactions of the Anglesey Antiquarian Society and Field Club*
T.C.H.S.	*Transactions of the Caernarvonshire Historical Society*
T.C.W.S.	*Transactions of the Cumberland and Westmorland Antiquarian and Archaeological Society*
T.D.G.S.	*Transactions of the Dumfriesshire and Galloway Natural History and Antiquarian Society*
T.H.S.C.	*Transactions of the Honourable Society of Cymmrodorion*
U.L.I.A.	*University of London Institute of Archaeology*
Y.C.	*Y Cymmrodor*
Z.C.P.	*Zeitschrift für celtische Philologie*

General Works of Reference, with Abbreviations

Note. Where only one work of an author is mentioned the author's name alone is generally cited. References to the works of Bede are confined to the *Historia Ecclesiastica*, and these are cited in the text briefly as Bede, and followed by the number of the Book and chapter of this work.

ANDERSON, A. O. and M. O. *Adomnán's Life of Columba* (Edinburgh, 1961)   Anderson A.L.C.

BLAIR, P. HUNTER. *An Introduction to Anglo-Saxon England* (Cambridge, 1956)   Blair A.S.E.

BROMWICH, R. *Trioedd Ynys Prydein, The Welsh Triads*
      Bromwich   Triads

Some Works of Reference and Sources

BRUCE-MITFORD, R. L. S. (Ed.) *Recent Archaeological Excavations in Britain* (London, 1956)   Bruce-Mitford R.A.E.B.

CHADWICK, H. M. and N. K. *The Growth of Literature*, Vol. I (Cambridge, 1932)   Chadwick *Growth*

CHADWICK, M. M. *Early Scotland* (Cambridge, 1949)
          Chadwick E.S.

CHADWICK, N. K. *Poetry and Letters in Early Christian Gaul* (London, 1955)   Chadwick P. and L.

CHADWICK, N. K. (Ed.) *Studies in Early British History* (Cambridge, 1943, reprinted 1959)   Chadwick S.E.B.H.
    (Ed.) *Studies in the Early British Church* (Cambridge, 1958)
          Chadwick S.E.B.C.
    The Age of the Saints in the Early Celtic Church (Oxford, 1961)
          Chadwick A.S.
    (Ed.) *Celt and Saxon: Studies in the Early British Border* (Cambridge, 1963)   Chadwick C.S.

COLLINGWOOD, R. G. and MYRES, J. N. L. *Roman Britain and the English Settlements* (Oxford, 1936)   Collingwood and Myres

DANIEL, G. E. 'Who are the Welsh?', *Proceedings of the British Academy*, Vol. XL (1954)   Daniel P.B.A.

ESPOSITO, M. 'The Knowledge of Greek in Ireland during the Middle Ages', *Studies* I (1911), 665 ff.   Esposito *Studies* I

FOX, C. and DICKINS, B. (Ed.) *The Early Cultures of North-West Europe* (Cambridge, 1950)   Fox and Dickins E.C.N.W.E.

FOX, A. In GRIMES, W. F. (Ed.) *A Hundred Years of Welsh Archaeology*, Cambrian Archaeological Association, 1846–1956   Fox H.Y.W.A.

FRERE, S. S. (Ed.) *Problems of the Iron Age in Southern Britain* (London, 1960)   U.L.I.A.

GRIMES, W. F. (Ed.) *Aspects of Archaeology in Britain and Beyond.* Essays presented to O. G. S. Crawford (London, 1951)
Grimes A.A.B.

HADDAN, A. W. and STUBBS, W. *Councils and Ecclesiastical Documents relating to Great Britain and Ireland,* 3 vols. (Vol. II in 2 parts) (Oxford, 1869–1878)   Haddan and Stubbs *Councils*

HARDEN, D. B. (Ed.) *Dark Age Britain. Studies Presented to E. T. Leeds* (London, 1956)   Harden D.A.B.

HENCKEN, H. O'N. *The Archaeology of Cornwall and Scilly* (London, 1932)   Hencken A.C.S.

JACKSON, K. 'The Britons of Southern Scotland', *Antiquity* XXIX, 77
Jackson B.S.S.
Language and History in Early Britain (Edinburgh, 1953)
Jackson L.H.E.B.

KENNEY, J. F. *Sources for the Early History of Ireland* (New York, 1929)
Kenney S.E.H.I.

KINVIG, R. H. *A History of the Isle of Man* (Liverpool, 1950)
Kinvig H.I.M.

LLOYD, J. E. *History of Wales,* 2 vols. (3rd ed. London, 1939)
Lloyd H.W.

LOT, F. *Nennius et l'Historia Brittonum,* 2 vols. (Paris, 1934)
Lot *Nennius*

MACALISTER, R. A. S. *Corpus Inscriptionum Insularum Celticarum,* Vol. I (Dublin, 1945), Vol. II (Dublin, 1949)   Macalister C.I.I.C.

NASH-WILLIAMS, V. E. *The Early Christian Monuments of Wales* (Cardiff, 1950) Nash-Williams E.C.M.W.

O'RAHILLY, C. *Ireland and Wales* (London, 1924) O'Rahilly I.W.

O'RAHILLY, T. F. *Early Irish History and Mythology* (Dublin, 1946) O'Rahilly E.I.H.M.

RICHMOND, I. A. and CRAWFORD, O. G. S. *The British Section of the Ravenna Cosmography* (Oxford, 1949) Richmond and Crawford B.S.R.C.

RODERICK, A. J. (Ed.) *Wales Through the Ages,* Vol. I (Llandybie, 1959) Roderick W.A.

STENTON, F. M. *Anglo-Saxon England* (Oxford, 1943) Stenton A.S.E.

STOKES, W. *Three Irish Glossaries* (Dublin, 1861) Stokes T.I.G.

WADE-EVANS, A. W. *Vitae Sanctorum Britanniae et Genealogiae* (Cardiff, 1944) Wade-Evans V.S.

WAINWRIGHT, F. T. *Archaeology and Place-Names and History* (London, 1962) Wainwright A.P.N.H.
Editor and contributor *The Northern Isles* (Edinburgh, 1962) Wainwright N.I.

WATSON, W. J. *History of the Celtic Place-Names of Scotland* (Edinburgh, 1926) Watson C.P.N.S.

WHEELER, R. E. M. *Prehistoric and Roman Wales* (Oxford, 1925) Wheeler P.R.W.

WILLIAMS, I. *Lectures on Early Welsh Poetry* Williams W.P.

M

Books and Articles relevant to the Chapters, with Abbreviations

Note. The majority of references to books will be found in the preceding list. Those cited in the lists relating to the following chapters are of more immediate reference, and here the title of a book is followed by its appropriate abbreviation where necessary.

CHAPTER I. *The End of Roman Britain*

ATKINSON, D. 'Classis Britannica', in *Historical Essays in Honour of James Tait* (ed. J. G. Edwards, V. H. Galbraith, E. F. Jacob, Manchester, 1933)   Atkinson C.B.

CHARLESWORTH, M.P. *The Lost Province* (Cardiff, 1949)
Charlesworth L.P.

CLARKE, R. R. *East Anglia* (London, 1960)   Clarke E.A.

COLLINGWOOD, R. G. and MYRES, J. N. L. *Roman Britain and the English Settlements* (Oxford, 1936)   Collingwood and Myres

FOX, C. *The Archaeology of the Cambridge Region* (Cambridge, 1923)
Fox A.C.R.

HAVERFIELD, F. *The Romanisation of Roman Britain* (4th ed., revised by G. Macdonald) (Oxford, 1923)
Haverfield and Macdonald R.R.B.

JACKSON, K. 'The Pictish Language' in Wainwright, *P.P.*, Appendix 'Common Gaelic', *P.B.A.* XXXVII (1951)   Jackson P.B.A.

LLOYD, J. E. *A History of Wales,* 2 vols. (London, 1911, 3rd ed. 1939)
Lloyd H.W.

NASH-WILLIAMS, V. E. *The Early Christian Monuments of Wales* (Cardiff, 1950)   Nash-Williams E.C.M.W.

RICHMOND, I. A. *Roman Britain* (Harmondsworth, 1955, new ed. 1963)
Richmond R.B.
'Roman Britain and Roman Military Antiquities', *Proceedings of the British Academy*, Vol. XLI (1955) Richmond P.B.A.
(Ed.) *Roman and Native in North Britain*, (London, 1958)
Richmond R.N.

RIVET, A. L. F. *Town and Country in Roman Britain* (London, 1958)
Rivet T.C.R.B.

SEECK, O., *Notitia Dignitatum* (Berlin, 1876) *Notitia Dignitatum*

SKENE, W. F. *Four Ancient Books of Wales*, 2 Vols., edited and translated (Edinburgh, 1868) Skene F.A.B.W.

WADE-EVANS, A. W. *Welsh Christian Origins* (Oxford, 1934)
Wade-Evans W.C.O.
Nennius's 'History of the Britons', together with 'The Annals of the Britons' and 'Court Pedigrees of Hywel the Good', also 'The Story of the Loss of Britain' (London, 1938) (English translation only)
Wade-Evans *Nennius*
Vitae Sanctorum Britanniae et Genealogiae, edited and translated (Cardiff, 1944) Wade-Evans V.S.B.G.

STARR, C. G. *The Roman Imperial Navy* (Ithaca N.Y., 1941)
Starr R.I.N.

WAINWRIGHT, F. T. (Ed.) *The Problem of the Picts* (Edinburgh, 1955)
Wainwright P.P.

WHEELER, R. E. M. *Prehistoric and Roman Wales* (Oxford, 1925)
Wheeler P.R.W.

WHITE, D. A. *Litus Saxonicum. The British Saxon Shore in Scholarship and History*, published by the State Historical Society of Wisconsin for

the Department of History, University of Wisconsin, Madison, 1961
White L.S.

CHAPTER II. *Celtic Rule in Britain*

BLAIR, P. HUNTER, *The Origins of Northumbria* (Gateshead-on-Tyne,
1948) Blair O.N.

CASPARI, C. P. *Briefe, Abhandlungen und Predigten* (Christiania, 1890);
[English translation by R. S. T. Haslehurst, *The Works of Fastidius*
(London, 1927)] Caspari *Briefe*

CHARLESWORTH, M. P. *The Lost Province* (Cardiff, 1949)
Charlesworth L.P.
FASTIDIUS, see Caspari.

LOOMIS, R. S. *Wales and the Arthurian Legend* (Cardiff, 1956)
Loomis W.A.L.
(Ed.) *Arthurian Literature in the Middle Ages* (Oxford, 1949)
Loomis A.L.

LOTH, J. *L'emigration bretonne en Armorique* (Paris, 1883)
Loth *L'emigration*

RICHMOND, I. A. 'Roman and Native in the Fourth Century A.D. and
After', being Chap. V of Richmond, *R.N.*

SAVORY, H. N. 'Excavations at Dinas Emrys, Beddgelert', Caernarvonshire', *A.C.* CIX (1961), 13. Savory A.C.

WAQUET, H. *Histoire de Bretagne* (Paris, 1958) Waquet H.B.

WHEELER, R. E. M. and T. V. *Report on the Excavation of the Prehistoric,
Roman, and Post-Roman Site in Lydney Park, Gloucestershire,* being No.

IX of the Reports of the Research Committee of the Society of Antiquaries of London (Oxford, 1932)   Wheeler *Lydney*

WRENN, C. L. 'Saxons and Celts in south-west Britain' (*T.H.S.C.*, 1959)   Wrenn T.H.S.C.

CHAPTER III. *The Foundation of the Kingdom of Scotland*

ANDERSON, A. O. *Early Sources of Scottish History*, 2 vols. (Edinburgh, 1922)   Anderson E.S.

ANDERSON, J. *Scotland in Early Christian Times*, 2 vols. (Edinburgh, 1881)   Anderson S.E.C.T.

ANDERSON, M. O. Articles on the texts and historical value of the lists of the Pictish and Scottish kings in the earliest times. Indispensable. *S.H.R.* XXVIII (1949) (Nos. 105 and 106); *ibid.* XXIX (1950)
                                                                     Anderson S.H.R.

CHADWICK, H. M. *Early Scotland* (Cambridge, 1949)
                                                                     Chadwick E.S.

DICKINSON, W. CROFT, DONALDSON, G. and MILNE, I. A. *A Source Book of Scottish History* (Edinburgh, 1952)   Dickinson S.B.

DICKINSON, W. CROFT, *Scotland from the Earliest Times to 1603*, Chaps. I–VIII   Dickinson S.E.T.

RICHMOND, I. A. (Ed.) *Roman and Native in North Britain*
                                                                     Richmond R.N.

SKENE, W. F. *Chronicles of the Picts and Scots* (Edinburgh, 1867)
                                                                     Skene P.S.
        Celtic Scotland, 3 vols. (Edinburgh, 1886–1890)   Skene C.S.

WAINWRIGHT, F. T. (Ed.) *The Problem of the Picts* (Edinburgh, 1955)
Wainwright P.P.
(Ed.) *The Northern Isles* (Edinburgh, 1961)   Wainwright N.I.

CHAPTER IV. *The Foundation of the Kingdom of Wales*

CHADWICK, H. M. and N. K. *The Growth of Literature,* Vol. I (Cambridge, 1932)   Chadwick *Growth*

CHADWICK, H. M. *Early Scotland* (Cambridge, 1949), Chap. X
Chadwick E.S.

LLOYD, J. E. *The Story of Ceredigion* (Cardiff, 1937)   Lloyd S.C.

RODERICK, A. J. (Editor and contributor) *Wales Through the Ages,* Vol. I (Llandybie, 1959)   Roderick W.A.

SKENE, W. F. *Chronicles of the Picts and Scots* (Edinburgh, 1857)
Skene P.S.
Four Ancient Books of Wales, 2 vols. (Edinburgh, 1868)
Skene F.A.B.W.
Celtic Scotland, 3 vols. (Edinburgh, 1886–1890)   Skene C.S.

STEVENSON, W. H. *Asser's Life of King Alfred* (Oxford, 1904; new impression with an article on recent work by D. Whitelock, Oxford, 1959). There is an English translation by J. A. Giles in his collection of *Six Old English Chronicles* (London, 1868), 43.

WILLIAMS, A. H. *An Introduction to the History of Wales,* Vol. I (Cardiff, 1941)   Williams H.W.

CHAPTER V. *Institutions and Way of Life*

ANDERSON, J. *Scotland in Pagan Times, The Iron Age* (Edinburgh, 1883)
Anderson s.i.a.

BINCHY, D. A. 'Sick Maintenance in Irish Law', *Ériu,* XII (1938)
Binchy *Ériu*
'The Linguistic and Historical Value of the Irish Law Tracts',
P.B.A. XXIX (1943)
Binchy p.b.a.
Chap. IV in M. Dillon, *Early Irish Society* (Dublin, 1954)
Binchy e.i.s.
'The Linguistic and Legal Archaisms in the Celtic Law-Books',
'Some Celtic Legal Terms', *Celtica* III (1955)   Binchy *Celtica*
Transactions of the Philological Society for 1959, published 1960
Binchy l.l.a.

BRAILSFORD, J. W. *The Mildenhall Treasure: A Provisional Handbook*
(British Museum, London, 1947)   Brailsford M.T.

CURLE, A. O. *The Treasure of Traprain Law* (Glasgow, 1923)
Curle t.t.

EDWARDS, J. G. 'The Normans and the Welsh March' (1956), *P.B.A.*
LXII   Edwards p.b.a.
Hywel Dda and the Welsh Lawbooks (Bangor, 1929)
Edwards h.d.w.l.

ELLIS, T. P. *Welsh Tribal Law and Custom in the Middle Ages,* I (Oxford
1926)   Ellis w.t.l.

FEACHAM, R. W. 'Fortifications'. See Wainwright, *P.P.,* 67.

LLOYD, J. E. *History of Wales,* I, Chaps. VIII, IX   Lloyd h.w.

MEGAW, B. R. S. 'The Monastery of St Maughold', *P.I.M.* (N.S. V,
1950), 169   Megaw p.i.m.

O'DELL, A. C. and others. 'The St Ninian's Isle Silver Hoard',
Antiquity XXXIII (1959) 241.   O'Dell *Antiquity*

O'DELL, A. C. and CAIN, A., *St Ninian's Isle Treasure* (Aberdeen
University Studies, Number 141., 1960)   O'Dell and Cain

O'RÍORDÁIN, S. P. 'Roman Material In Ireland,' *P.R.I.A.* LI, Section
C, No. 3 (Dublin, 1947)   O'Ríordáin P.R.I.A.

REES, J. *South Wales and the March* (Oxford, 1924)   Rees S.W.M.

RICHARDS, MELVILLE. *The Laws of Hywel Dda* (*The Book of Blegywryd*)
(Liverpool, 1954), English translation, with Introduction
                                    Melville Richards L.H.D.

RYAN, J. *Irish Monasticism* (Dublin, 1931)   Ryan I.M.
'Learning in Irish Monasteries', *J.R.S.A.I.* LXXX (1950)
                                            Ryan L.I.M.

SEEBOHM, F. *The Tribal System in Wales* (2nd ed., London, 1904)
                                            Seebohm T.S.W.
Tribal Custom in Anglo-Saxon Law (London, 1911), 298
                                            Seebohm T.C.A.L.

THURNEYSEN, R. *Studies in Early Irish Law*   Thurneysen S.E.I.L.

WADE-EVANS, A. W. *Welsh Medieval Law* (Oxford, 1909), Welsh
text, English translation, and Introduction   Wade-Evans W.M.L.

WILSON, D. M. and BLUNT, C. E. 'The Trewhiddle Hoard', *Archaeologia* XCVIII (1961), 75.   Wilson and Blunt T.H.

CHAPTER VI. *Literature*

BELL, H. I. *The Development of Welsh Poetry* (Oxford, 1936)
                                            Bell D.W.P.

BROMWICH, R. *Trioedd Ynys Prydein, The Welsh Triads,* edited with Introduction, Translation and Commentary by Rachel Bromwich (Cardiff, 1961)   Bromwich *Triads*

CHADWICK, M. M. and N. K. *The Growth of Literature,* Vol. I (Cambridge, 1932)   Chadwick *Growth*

ELLIS, T. P. and LLOYD, J. *The Mabinogion.* English translation (Oxford, 1929)   Ellis and Lloyd *Mabinogion*

GRUFFYDD, W. *Math vab Mathonwy* (Cardiff, 1928)   Gruffyd *Math*

JACKSON, K. *Studies in Early Celtic Nature Poetry* (Cambridge, 1935)
                              Jackson S.E.C.N.P.
Early Welsh Gnomic Poems (Cardiff, 1935)   Jackson E.W.G.P.
Review of I. Williams, Gododdin, *Antiquity* XIII (1939), 25
                              Jackson *Antiquity*
'Notes on the Ogam Inscriptions of Southern Britain' in
                              Fox and Dickins (See p. 171)
A Celtic Miscellany (London, 1951)   Jackson C.M.
Early Cultures in North-Western Europe (Cambridge, 1950)
                              Jackson E.C.N.-W.E.

JONES, G. and JONES, T. *Mabinogion,* English translation (London, 1949)   Jones *Mabinogion*

JONES, G., MORGAN, J. T. and WILLIAMS, I. *The Saga of Llywarch the Old* (printed in Great Britain at the Golden Cockerel Press, 1955)
                              Jones, Morgan and Williams S.L.O.

LOTH, J. *Les Mabinogion,* translation by J. Loth, 2 vols. (Paris, 1913). This is fully annotated and also contains appendices which include a selection of the Triads, the genealogies of MS, Harl. 3859 and the text of the *Annales Cambriae.*

MacCANA, P. *Branwen Daughter of Llyr* (Cardiff, 1938)
MacCana   *Branwen*

PARRY, T. *A History of Welsh Literature,* translated from the Welsh by
H. Idris Bell (Oxford, 1955)   Parry H.W.L.
The Oxford Book of Welsh Verse (Oxford, 1962)   Parry O.B.W.V.

SKENE, W. F. *The Four Ancient Books of Wales*. Vol. I, English translation; Vol. II, Welsh text (Edinburgh, 1868)   Skene F.A.B.W.

WILLIAMS, G. *An Introduction to Welsh Poetry* (London, 1953)
Williams I.W.P.
The Burning Tree, English translations of Early Welsh Poems
(London, 1956)   Williams B.T.

WILLIAMS, SIR IFOR *Pedeir Keinc y Mabinogi,* Welsh text (Cardiff, 1930)
Williams P.K.
'The Poems of Llywarch Hen', *P.B.A.* XVIII (1932)
Williams P.B.A.
Canu Llywarch Hen, Welsh text (Cardiff, 1935)
Williams C.Ll.H.
Canu Aneirin, Welsh text (Cardiff, 1938)   Williams C.A.
Lectures on Early Welsh Poetry (Dublin, 1944)   Williams E.W.P.
Armes Prydein, Welsh text (Cardiff, 1955)   Williams A.B.
Canu Taliesin, Welsh text (Cardiff, 1960)   Williams C.T.

CHAPTER VII. *Art and Inscriptions*

ALLEN, J. ROMILLY, *The Early Christian Monuments of Scotland* (Edinburgh, 1893)   Allen E.C.M.S.

ANDERSON, J. Introduction to Allen (as above), being the Rhind
Lectures (Edinburgh 1892)   Anderson R.A.

CLAPHAM, W. 'Notes on the Origins of Hiberno-Saxon Art', *Antiquity* VIII (1934)   Clapham *Antiquity*

CRUDEN, S. *The Early Christian and Pictish Monuments of Scotland* (Edinburgh, Stationery Office, 1957)   Cruden E.C.P.M.S.

CURLE, A. O. *The Treasure of Traprain* (Glasgow, 1923)   Curle T.T.

CURLE, C. L. 'The Chronology of the Early Christian Monuments of Scotland', Curle, *P.S.A.S.* LXXIV (1–40), 60.
Curle P.S.A.S.

DIACK, F. C. *The Inscriptions of Pictland* (Aberdeen, 1944)
Diack I.P.

HENCKEN, H. O'N. *The Archaeology of Cornwall and Scilly* (London, 1932)   Hencken A.C.S.

HENDERSON, I. M. 'The Origin Centre of the Pictish Symbol Stones', *P.S.A.S.* XCI (1957–8), 44.   Henderson P.S.A.S.

HENRY, F. *Irish Art in the Early Christian Period* (London, 2nd ed., 1940)   Henry I.A.E.C.P.

JACKSON, K. 'The Pictish Language', being Chap. VI of Wainwright, *P.P.* (see below)

KERMODE, P. M. C. *Manx Crosses* (London, 1907)   Kermode M.C.

KINVIG, R. H. *A History of the Isle of Man* (Liverpool, 1950)
Kinvig H.I.M.

LANGDON, A. G. *Old Cornish Crosses* (Truro, 1896)
Langdon O.C.C.

O'DELL. See Chapter V

RADFORD, C. A. R. 'The Early Christian Monuments of Scotland', *Antiquity* XVI (1942), 1   Radford *Antiquity*

'Castle Dore,' *J.R.I.C.*, New Series I, Appendix, 1951
Radford J.R.I.C.
Whithorn and Kirkmadrine, Ministry of Works Official Guide-book
(Edinburgh, 1957) Radford W. and K.

STEVENSON, R. B. K. 'Pictish Art', being Chap. V of *P.P.* (see below
Wainwright) Stevenson P.A.

STUART, J. *The Sculptured Stones of Scotland,* 2 vols. Vol. I, Aberdeen,
1856; Vol. II, Edinburgh, 1867 Stuart s.s.s.

TALBOT RICE, D. *English Art 871–1100* (Oxford, 1952)
Talbot Rice E.A.

WAINWRIGHT, F. T. (Ed.) *The Problem of the Picts* (Edinburgh, 1955)
Wainwright P.P.

CHAPTER VIII. *The Church*

ANDERSON, A. O. and M. O. *Adomnán's Life of Columba* (Edinburgh
and London, 1961) Anderson *Columba*

ANDERSON, J. *Scotland in Early Christian Times,* 2 vols. (Edinburgh,
1881) Anderson s.e.c.t.

ASHLEY, ANNE. *The Church in the Isle of Man* (London and York,
1958) Ashley c.i.m.

BARING-GOULD, S. and FISHER, JOHN *The Lives of the British Saints,*
4 vols. (London, 1907–1913) Baring-Gould and Fisher L.B.S.

BIELER, L. *The Life and Legend of St Patrick* (Dublin, 1949)
Bieler L.L.P.

Some Works of Reference and Sources

BINCHY, D. A. 'Patrick and his Biographers', *S.H.* No. 2 (Dublin 1962), 1–173

BOWEN, E. G. *The Settlements of the Early Saints in Wales* (Cardiff, 1954)   Bowen *Settlements*

BURY, J. B. *The Life of St Patrick* (London, 1905)   Bury L.P.

CARNEY, J. *The Problem of St Patrick* (Dublin, 1961)   Carney P.S.P.

CHADWICK, N. K. *Poetry and Letters in Early Christian Gaul* (London, 1955)   Chadwick P.L.
  The Age of the Saints in the Early Celtic Church (Oxford, 1961)   Chadwick A.S.

CHOPE, R. P. *The Book of Hartland* (Torquay, 1940)   Chope B.H.

COLGRAVE, B. *The Life of Bishop Wilfrid by Eddius Stephanus*   Colgrave *Eddius*
  Two Lives of Saint Cuthbert (Cambridge, 1940)   Colgrave *St Cuthbert*
  Felix's Life of Saint Guthlac (Cambridge, 1956)   Colgrave *St Guthlac*

COOPER-MARSDIN, A. *History of the Islands of the Lérins* (Cambridge, 1913)   Cooper-Marsdin H.I.L.

DE PAOR, M. and L. *Early Christian Ireland* (London, 1958)   de Paor E.C.I.

DOBLE, REV. CANON G. H. *St Iltut* (Cardiff, 1944)   Doble S.I.
  The Saints of Cornwall (Chatham, 1960)   Doble S.C.

FAWTIER, R. *La vie de Saint Samson* (Paris, 1912)   Fawtier V.S.

GOUGAUD, DOM LOUIS. *Christianity in Celtic Lands,* translated from the author's MS by Maud Joynt (London, 1932)
Gougaud C.C.L.

GROSJEAN, REV. PAUL, S. J. *Bollandist,* 'Edition et Commentaire du Catalogus Sanctorum Hibereniae secundum diversa tempora ou De tribus Ordinibus Sanctorum Hiberniae', *A.B.* LXXIII (1955)
Grosjean A.B.

HALLIDAY, F. E. *A History of Cornwall* (London, 1959)
Halliday H.C.

JOHNS, C. N. 'The Celtic Monasteries of North Wales', *T.C.H.S* XXI (1960)
Johns T.C.H.S.

KENNEY, F. J. *The Sources for the Early History of Ireland,* I. Ecclesiastical (New York, 1929)
Kenney S.E.H.I.

LLAN-DAV BOOK OF, Text reproduced by J. G. Evans and J. Rhys (Oxford, 1893); also W. J. Rees, *Liber Landavensis* (Llandovery, 1840) (with English translation).

LAWLOR, H. C. *The Monastery of St Mochaoi of Nendrum* (Belfast, 1925)
Lawlor *Nendrum*

MACQUEEN, J. *St Ninia* (Edinburgh, 1961)   MacQueen *St Ninia*

MEATES, G. W. *Lullingstone Roman Villa* (London, 1955)
Meates L.R.V.

NISBET, H. C. and GAILEY, R. A. 'A Survey of the Antiquities of North Rona', *Arch. J.* CXVI (1961), 87.   Nisbet and Gailey

NOCK, SISTER F. C. *Vita Sancti Fructuosi* (Washington, 1946)
Nock V.S.F.

RADFORD, C. A. R. *The Early Christian and Norse Settlements of Birsay* (Ministry of Works Official Guide-book, Edinburgh, 1959)
Radford *Birsay*
'The Church in Somerset to 1100', *P.S.A. Som.* CVI (1962)
Radford C.S.

REEVES, W. *The Life of St Columba* (Dublin, 1857) Reeves L.S.C.

TAYLOR, T. *Life of St Samson of Dol*, English translation (London, 1925) Taylor L.S.D.

THOMPSON, E. A. 'The Origin of Christianity in Scotland', *S.H.R.* XXXVII (1958) Thompson S.H.R.

TOYNBEE, J. M. C. 'Christianity in Roman Britain', *J.B.A.A.* (Third Series, XVI, 1953) Toynbee J.B.A.A.

WADE-EVANS, A. W. *Welsh Christian Origins* (Oxford, 1934)
Wade-Evans W.C.O.
Vitae Sanctorum Britanniae et Genealogiae (contains the texts and translations of many of the principal Welsh saints, edited and translated, Cardiff, 1944) Wade-Evans V.S.B.G.

WALKER, G. S. M. *Sancti Columbani Opera* (Dublin, 1957)
Walker S.C.O.

WILLIAMS, H. *Christianity in Early Britain* (Oxford, 1912)
Williams C.E.B.

ZIMMER, H. *The Celtic Church in Britain and Ireland*, translated by A. Meyer (London, 1902) Zimmer C.C.

Sources of Illustrations

Acknowledgment for photographs used in the plates is made to the following: Ministry of Works, Photographic Department, London, 2–5; Ministry of Public Buildings and Works, Edinburgh, 8, 9, 15, 24, 39, 40, 42–50; Trustees of the British Museum, 20; Royal Commission on Ancient Monuments in Wales and Monmouthshire, Aberystwyth, 18, 19, 23, 26, 62; National Museum of Antiquities of Scotland, Edinburgh, 27–32, 55; National Museum of Wales, 10, 33 (the latter photograph by Mr Leslie Alcock); Air Ministry, London, and Committee for Aerial Photography, Cambridge (photographs by J. K. St Joseph, Crown Copyright Reserved), 1, 16, 34, 65–67; by courtesy of the Manx Museum, 37, 38, 41, 63, 64; the Bodleian Library, Oxford, 6; Professor A. C. O'Dell, Department of Geography, University of Aberdeen, 51–54; Mr A. Cain of the Anatomy Department, University of Aberdeen (for the photographs taken by permission of Professor O'Dell, as above, and for the photograph taken by Mr Cain from a slide kindly lent by Dr W. Douglas Simpson, after which the line drawing for figure 33 was made); the Iona Community, 56, 57; Dr Harold Taylor, Vice-Chancellor of the University of Keele, 21, 59, 60; Sir Mortimer Wheeler and the Society of Antiquaries, London, 7; Cambridge University Library, 58 (from a photograph by the Earl of Dunraven in *Notes on Irish Architecture*); Mr Edwin Smith, 25; Mr Charles Woolf, Newquay, 35, 36; J. B. White Ltd, Dundee, 13, 14; John Leng and Co. Ltd, Dundee, 12 (photograph by the late R. M. Adam); Valentine and Sons Ltd, Dundee, 61.

The line drawings, which are from a wide variety of sources, are the work of Mr Michael Langham Rowe of Cambridge, except figures 4, 18, 33, 35, which were drawn by Mr Michael Spink of Thames & Hudson. The maps were drawn by Mr H. A. Shelley of Cambridge.

1

4

5

.F·L.

INTALL.

COMORD.

.PR.

othona.

Dubris.

Lemaniis.

Branoduno

Gariannn

Regulbi.

Rutupis.

Anderidos.

Portuaduru.

6

7

9

10

13

14

15

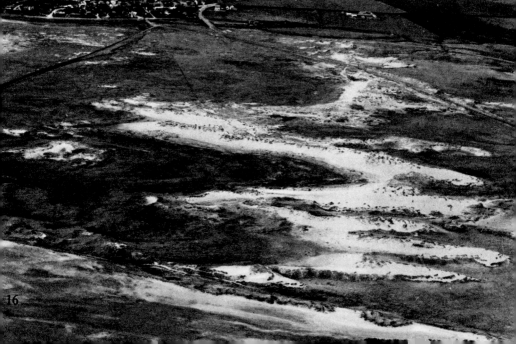

16

17

18

19

20

21

2

23

4

25

26

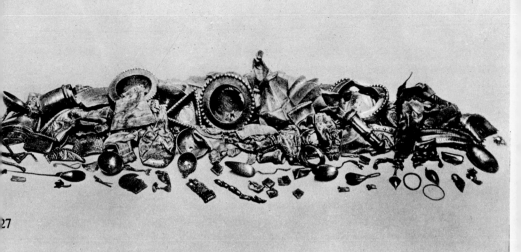

27

28

29

30

31

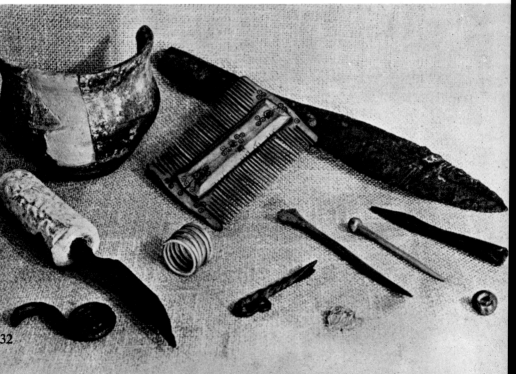

32

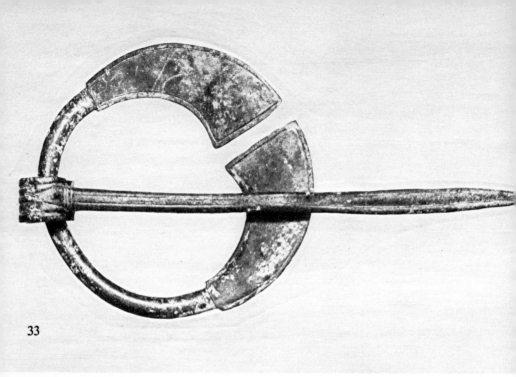

33

34

35

36

37

38

39

41

40

43a

43b

44

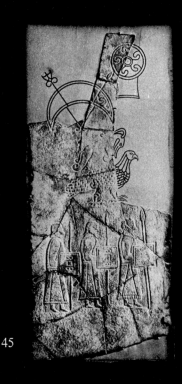

45

46a

46b

47

48

49

50

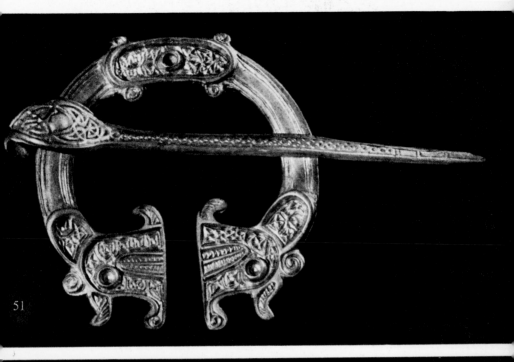

51

52　　　　　　　　　　　53

54

55

56

57

58

59

60

61

63

64

65

66

67

1 Bartlow Barrows from the air. Remains of a cemetery of considerable size, forming two parallel rows of burial mounds, the western row probably once consisting of five small barrows, two of which still remain; the eastern of four steep-sided conical mounds, the largest 40 ft high and 145 ft in diameter. Early excavations produced rich material of the Roman period, and the barrows are believed to be the family graves of East Anglian British nobles of the Roman period. See Fox, *A.C.R.*, p. 191 f., 197 ff.

2, 3 Burgh Castle (*Garrianonum*) in Suffolk, one of the Saxon shore forts, seen from the air (2) and from the ground (3).

4 Portchester. Saxon shore fort, built by the Romans at the end of the third or in the early fourth century. The greater part of the original Roman building still stands, though in places re-faced and repaired, and adapted to the needs of a medieval castle and monastery. The Roman fortress encloses an area of about 9 acres, planned as a square, with two gateways, in the middle of the east and west sides, and having twenty bastions, fourteen of which still remain. Our picture shows the east or water gate, in its outer part of fourteenth-century date, but on the original Roman foundation. See Sir Charles Peers, *Portchester Castle* (London, H.M.S.O., 1953, reprinted 1962).

5 Portchester. The same Saxon shore fort. The eastern water gate, taken from within. The inner half, which projects into the bailey, has been thought to be Roman on account of its round arch and voussoirs; but it is more probably Norman.

6 *Notitia Dignitatum*. A page from the manuscript in the Bodleian Library at Oxford (cf. p. 31 above). The captions to the little buildings claim that each represents one of the 'Forts of the Saxon Shore', and the title of this page in the manuscript would assign them to the command of the Count of the Saxon Shore in Britain.

7　Bronze dog, 4 in. long, found at the site of the Romano-British temple in Lydney Park, Gloucestershire, at a small distance from the wall of the temple. Probably late fourth century. Perhaps represents an Irish wolf-hound. (Cf. p. 35 above.)

8　Dumbarton Rock (Altclut), the ancient fortified stronghold of the North British dynasty of Ceredig Gwledig, and later of Rhydderch Hen, at the mouth of the Clyde. It guarded the western end of the Antonine Wall against the tribes to the north.

9　The Catstone, Midlothian. Rough inscribed boulder *in situ*; early post-Roman memorial stone, with Latin lettering and formula. Anderson, *S.E.C.T.* (Second Series) p. 247; Macalister, *C.I.I.C.* I, no. 510.

10　Castell Dwyran stone, Carmarthenshire. Latin and ogam inscriptions (cf. p. 41 above). Found in the churchyard as above, now in the Carmarthen museum. Mid sixth century. Nash-Williams, *E.C.M.W.*, pl. III, fig. 138, p. 107.

11　Dunseverick, on the north coast of Co. Antrim, now a ruined medieval castle, the site of the dynasty of Dálriada. (Cf. p. 59 above.)

12　Pass of Drumochter, over the Mounth, between Badenoch and Atholl, separating the watersheds of the Rivers Spey and Tay. The main route overland from the Northern to the Southern Picts, it was very desolate, and is described in a medieval survey as 'passagium pessimum, sine cibo'. (Cf. p. 53 above.)

13　Schiehallion, Perthshire. The name means 'The magical, or super-natural hill of the Caledonians'. It overlooks the Tay and the Tummel, in the heart of the Perthshire Highlands.

14　Dunollie, Oban, Argyll; site of the stronghold of the Cenél Loairn, a rival branch of the same fifth-century intrusive Irish dynasty as the Cenél Gabráin (see note 17).

15　Traprain Law, Dunpelder, East Lothian, a large Iron Age hill-fort covering 32 acres, and apparently occupied continuously through and after the Roman period, till the fourth century A.D. In medieval tradition it figures as the site of the king of Lothian, and the home of his daughter, St Kentigern's mother.

16 Air view showing the sandy flats between Aberffraw, Anglesey, the palace of the princes of Gwynedd, and Llangadwaladr, their royal cemetery, 2 miles to the south. It will be noticed how suitable the terrain is for the exercising of horses. The modern road can just be traced in the right-hand corner. It is interesting to reflect that the distance between the palace and the royal cemetery is about the same as that between Mathrafal, the palace of the princes of Powys, and their royal cemetery at Meifod in Montgomeryshire; and that between Dinefwr, the traditional royal seat of the princes of Deheubarth (cf. p. 65 above), and Llandeilo Fawr, their principal church.

17 Dunadd, Argyll, a rock citadel with additional stone ramparts, in the midst of Crinan Moss. It is believed to have been from the fifth century the stronghold of the Cenél Gabráin, the branch of the intrusive Irish dynasty from Irish Dálriada which eventually became dominant in Scotland (cf. p. 60 above).

18 Llangadwaladr, Anglesey. Latin inscription in five lines reading vertically downwards, surmounted by a small inscribed Latin cross. Now inside the church, built horizontally into the north wall of the nave. Sixth century. Nash-Williams, *E.C.M.W.*, pl. VII, no. 13, pp. 55, 56, fig. 21. (Cf. pp. 70 f. above.)

19 Llansadwrn, Anglesey. Latin inscription in four (?) lines reading horizontally (?). Found in churchyard, now built into north chancel wall inside the church. Believed to commemorate the founder of the church and his wife. *Hic bea(tu)s Saturninus se(pultus) (j)acit et sua sa(ncta) (?) conju(n)x.* Sixth century. Nash-Williams, *E.C.M.W.*, pl. VII, no. 32.

20 Hywel Dda's silver penny. The first silver coin attributed to a Welsh king. On the obverse is the legend *Howæl rex* and on the reverse Gillys, the name of a Chester moneyer. It will be noticed that Gillys is an Irish name.

N*

21 Cross of Muiredach, Monasterboice, Co. Louth. A wheel cross, all the figures being carved in high relief. In the lowest register two cats are seen licking their kittens. The inscription on the cross states that it was given by one Muiredach, believed to be the abbot of Monasterboice who died in A.D. 923. (Cf. p. 88 above.)

22 The Rivals (Welsh *Yr Eifl*), three impressive mountain peaks to the north of Nevin Bay in the peninsula of Lleyn, Caernarvonshire. On the easternmost of these peaks is the Iron Age fort, Tre'r Ceiri, 'City of Giants'. (Cf. p. 91 above.)

23 Tre'r Ceiri, as seen from the air; an Iron Age fortress crowning the most easterly of the three peaks of Yr Eifl on the north coast of the Lleyn peninsula in Caernarvonshire. The interior of the main enclosures is occupied by about 150 huts of very varied shapes. The pottery found in recent excavations was almost all Roman, and the evidence as a whole points to continuous occupation from the foundation of the fort until some time in the fourth century or later. See A. H. A. Hogg, in *Arch. J.* CXVII (1961), 1 ff.

24 The Broch of Mousa, Shetland, external view. This is the tallest and the best preserved of the brochs. (Cf. p. 92 above.)

25 The Broch of Dun Carloway, Isle of Lewis, internal section, showing stepped galleries. (Cf. p. 92 above.)

26 Circular hut (Hut 2) at Din Lligwy, seen from the east. Din Lligwy is a famous Romano-British walled hut-group near the north-east coast of Anglesey. The remains consist of two circular and seven rectangular buildings, with two rectangular foundations outside. The site is near the important copper mines worked in Roman times, and was probably the home of a local chieftain of importance. See the publication of the *Inventory of Anglesey* (1937), issued by the Royal Commission on Historical Monuments in Wales and Monmouthshire, p. 134. (Cf. p. 94 above.)

27 The treasure as found in 1919 during excavations on Traprain Law. It is certainly loot, most likely from Gaul, with some items probably of

Mediterranean origin, and a few the property of Teutonic immigrants. (Cf. p. 95 above.)

28   Goblets, two complete, and portions of others, from the Traprain Law treasure. The interior of the top left-hand goblet still retains its original gilding, and on the underside of the base are scratched the three letters C O N. See A. O. Curle, *The Treasure of Traprain*, p. 29. (See also p. 95 above.)

29   Massive silver chains, probably originally about 16 in. long, weighing from 97½ to 22 oz. The penannular terminal fasteners in two cases are engraved with Pictish symbols, originally inlaid in red enamel. They were probably neck ornaments. In addition to those shown, three more are known. They were found singly, not in hoards, and from widely divergent parts of Scotland, but none from elsewhere. Cf. *P.S.A.S.* 1954–56; Anderson, *S.E.C.T.*, II (1881), 42 ff. (Cf. p. 130 above.)

30   Hunterston Brooch, found near Largs, Ayrshire, in 1826. 4¾ in. in diameter. It is made of silver, partially (?) gilt, with gold filigree and granulation, and amber insets. On the back is a runic inscription finely incised, recording the names of two of the former owners. The art is Celtic, of exceptionally fine quality, and the original provenance probably the Inner Hebrides. Date uncertain, perhaps early eighth century, but if the inscription is of the same date it may be considerably later.

31   The Monymusk Reliquary, a wooden box enclosed in bronze, *c.* A.D. 700, now in the National Museum of Antiquities in Edinburgh. It is believed to be the relic of St Columba frequently referred to in ancient charters as the *Brecbennoch*, and as having the function of being carried into battle along with the other relics of the saint, notably his Psalter, the *Cathach*, and his crosier, the *Cath Bhuaidh*. The decoration consists of engraving on the metal combined with red and yellow enamel, and in parts of gilt bronze with a deeply cut background. The engraved design resembles that of the MS. of the *Book of Durrow*. Cf. Anderson, *S.E.C.T.* I, 241 ff.; Henry, *I.A.E.C.P.*, 70 f.; Stevenson in Wainwright, *P.P.*, p. 108 ff.

32 Contents of a circular house site on Buston Crannog, North Ayrshire. Apparently a site *c.* A.D. 700 of a single period, despite fragments of Roman glass. Among other interesting objects are a Frankish pottery cup, a gold spiral finger-ring, and an Anglo-Saxon gold coin, perhaps an early forgery, of the seventh century, showing contact with England. See Sutherland, *Anglo-Saxon Gold Coinage*, p. 88, coin 55.

33 Penannular silver brooch from Pant-y-Saer, Anglesey, excavated by C. W. Phillips in 1932–3. Its closest parallels are from the coastal regions of Scotland, and range from the fourth to the sixth century. This brooch probably dates from the later part of the period. It is now in the National Museum of Wales, Cardiff. See Phillips, *A.C.* LXXXIX (1934), 1 ff.

34 Air view of Tintagel Head and Castle, Cornwall. A Celtic monastery, believed to date from *c.* 500, excavated in 1933 and 1934. Four graves of the monks cut out of the solid rock were found. Pottery found on the site suggests connection with the south of Gaul at this date. See Radford, *A.C.* XV (1935), 401 ff.; CXI (1962), 7 ff: Cf. further *Tintagel Castle* (Official Guide, H.M.S.O., London, 1939).

35 Cunomorus Stone, also known as the Menabilly Stone, near Fowey, Cornwall. A pillar over 7 ft high, roughly squared, and carved with a Latin inscription in two vertical lines. On the back is a T-cross in relief. ؟ Sixth century. Macalister, *C.I.I.C.* I, no. 487; Radford, *J.R.I.C.*, N.S. I (1951), p. 117; Hencken, *C. S.*, p. 222. (Cf. p. 120 above.)

36 Cardinham Cross, Cornwall, in the churchyard at Cardinham, near Bodmin. The most elaborately decorated of the Cornish crosses. ؟ Tenth century. Langdon, no. 3, facing p. 356; Hencken, *C.S.*, fig. 50, p. 274.

37 Calf of Man Crucifixion slab, Isle of Man. Broken slab with relief sculpture of the Crucifixion. Kermode, pl. XVI, pp. 123, 125; Megaw, *J.M.M.* VI (1958), pl. 236. See also Talbot Rice, *E.A.*, 104. (Cf. p. 121 above.)

38 Crux Guriat, Isle of Man. From Port-y-Vullen, Maughold. Incised cross with some slight relief. Early ninth century. Of special historical importance. Kermode, pl. XV, p. 121. (Cf. p. 121 above.)

39 Meigle, Perthshire. Sculptured cross-slab. The central figure probably represents Daniel in the lions' den. Note the absence of stirrups on the horsemen, and the housing on the rear horse. Centaur below.

40 Meigle, Perthshire. Incised slab. Note the receding planes of the sculpture. (Cf. p. 137 above.)

41 Inscription of Branhui, recently unearthed in the churchyard of Maughold, Isle of Man. The inscription, about 22 in. wide, commemorates a certain Branhui, evidently a monk of the community of Maughold, bearing a Welsh name, who is stated here to have 'led off water to this place'. From this it would appear that he provided the brethren with a supply of running water for domestic use, and traces of a stone-lined conduit found in the same churchyard are interesting confirmation of the inscription. It dates from *c.* 800. Cf. Megaw, 'The Monastery of Maughold', *P.I.M.*, N.S. V, no. 2 (1950), 170. (Cf. p. 94 above.)

42 Brandsbutt, Aberdeenshire. Incised boulder with symbols and ogam inscription. ? Eighth or ninth century. Jackson, 'The Pictish Language' in Wainwright, *P.P.*, 141. (Cf. p. 128 above.)

43 Glamis Stone at the Manse. (*a*) Front. Cross, in high relief, filled with interlace design. Symbols and human figures, all in low relief, occupy the spaces between the arms of the cross. The background has been smoothed. (*b*) Back of the same stone. The original surface has been retained in the rough, and the design adapted to the natural irregularities of the stone. The design consists of three symbols only—serpent, fish, and mirror. See Cruden, *Early Christian and Pictish Monuments of Scotland*, pl. 5 and 6.

44 Hilton of Cadboll, Ross-shire. Upright slab, elaborately carved with advanced skill. Note the ornamental border with inhabited vine-scroll, a rare feature in Pictish work; also symbols filled with interlace. Vigorous hunting scene below. The surface of the reverse, which probably bore a hunting scene, is wholly destroyed. (Cf. p. 137 above.)

45 The Birsay symbol stone, from the Brough of Birsay, Orkney. The sculptured stones and large cemetery are associated with the ruins of a small church which has been identified under the Norse cathedral, and which were surrounded by a cashel wall. An early cross and fragmentary ogam inscription from the same cemetery suggest a monastic settlement of the seventh or eighth century. Radford, *Early Christian and Norse Settlements at Birsay, Orkney*, H.M.S.O., 1959.

46 Aberlemno, Angus. Cross-slab, with narrative scene on the reverse. (*a*) Front; (*b*) reverse. Stevenson, in Wainwright, *P.P.*, pl. 8, p. 113. (Cf. p. 137 above.)

47 Papil stone, one of a number found at an important early ecclesiastical site on the island of Burra, perhaps the chief monastic centre of the southern part of Mainland, Shetland. See Wainwright, *N.I.*, 95, 114.

48 Dunfallandy, Perthshire. Sculptured cross-slab, reverse panel. Note the intermingling of symbols and realistic figures carved in relief and incised properties. (Cf. p. 137 above.)

49, 50 St Andrews sarcophagus shrine, St Andrews, Fife. Front view (49) and detail (50). C. L. Curle, p. 98; Allen, *E.C.M.S.*, fig. 365, front (no. 1), p. 350. Cf. further Radford, *Antiquity* XVI, p. 9. (Cf. p. 139 above.)

51-54 Silver hoard from St Ninian's Isle, Shetland, discovered in 1958. See O'Dell, *Antiquity* XXXIII (1959). Brooch (51); bowl, underside (52), detail (53); spoon with dog's-head design (54). (Cf. pp. 96, 139 above.)

55 Part of silver dish in the Traprain Law treasure. (See also Plates 27 and 28, and cf. p. 95 above.)

56 Iona, Argyllshire, the site of St Columba's monastic foundation. The view shows the site of the later medieval abbey, recently rebuilt, and looks across the Sound to the Island of Mull. (Cf. p. 145 above.)

57 St Martin's Cross, Iona. Free-standing wheel-headed high cross of Irish type. Ninth or tenth century. (Cf. p. 124 above.)

58 Inishmurray, a small island some 4 miles off the coast of Sligo, recently depopulated. It contains the remains of a monastic settlement of approximately the same period as Skellig Michael (59, 60), but is not so fully preserved. There are the remains of three or four beehive dwellings and a contemporary church and a small oratory. Of great interest is the massive stone monastic enclosure wall, or *cashel*, the most complete remaining today in Ireland, 15 ft thick at the base and about 13 ft high. It has several wall chambers, and one or two structural enclosures. A number of internal flights of steps give access from ground level to the top of the cashel, just as in Staigue Fort in Co. Kerry and the Grínán Ailech, Co. Donegal. A number of early grave slabs and signs of pilgrimage stations survive.

9, 60 Skellig Michael (in Irish, Sceilg Mhichíl), an early Celtic monastic site, probably of the sixth or seventh century, on a precipitous bare rock some 700 ft high, quite isolated, in the Atlantic, 8 miles from the most south-westerly headlands of Ireland. It is the most perfectly preserved of all the island sanctuaries of the Age of the Saints, its six beehive-shaped cells and two little oratories being still completely intact, including the corbelled roofs. There is a tiny burial plot, and there are some slabs incised with crosses. Plate 59 shows two of the beehive-shaped cells, 60 the stairway (some 600 steps) leading to the monastery.

61 Bardsey Island, off the western tip of the Lleyn Peninsula, Caernarvonshire, by tradition the final resting-place of 20,000 saints. This view is taken from St Mary's Well at the end of the Pilgrim's Way, the point of departure for Bardsey in olden times. (Cf. p. 146 above.)

62 Early Celtic church, now embedded in the present twelfth-century church, on Ynys Seiriol (also known as Priestholm or Puffin Island), off the south-eastern tip of Anglesey. The earlier foundations measured 5 ft square and had a stone barrel vault and a sharply pointed roof, the lines of both of which can be seen against the east wall of the tower. The church stands within the cashel wall of an early Celtic monastic settlement of about three-quarters of an acre. The oldest part of the cashel wall probably dates from the seventh century, and grouped along it traces have been found of three or four rectangular cells, measuring

about 10 in. by 10 to 25 in. See *Inventory of Anglesey* (1937), Royal Commission on Ancient Monuments in Wales and Monmouthshire, 141 ff.; Radford, in *A.C.* CXI (1962), 28. (Cf. p. 146 above.)

63 Spooyt Vane Keeill, Isle of Man. One of the 200 *keeills* or small Celtic places of worship dating from the seventh to the fifteenth centuries. They are simple structures, rectangular in plan without apse or rounded end and with no obvious division between nave and chancel, the area being only some 12 ft long by 8 or 9 ft wide. Occasionally a small additional chamber is attached, possibly a sacristy. (Cf. p. 145 above.)

64 Inscription at Kirk Maughold, Isle of Man, stating in runic letters that it was 'carved by Iuan the Priest'. Below this statement is the alphabet in both runic and ogam letters. The stone is a natural slab, but with the inscription on the smooth face, and measures about 1 ft each way. See Kermode, *M.C.*, p. 213; Macalister, *C.I.I.C.* I, p. 483 (cf. p. 144 above). The slab was found embedded in the wall during repairs to the present church. It doubtless refers to Iuan the priest mentioned in an inscription from Cornadale, also in the Isle of Man.

65 Hoddom, Dumfriesshire, from the air. Foundations of a chapel and burial ground traditionally dedicated to St Kentigern (cf. p. 147 above). A crozier excavated at no great distance may possibly support the tradition that Hoddom was the saint's first bishopric.

66 Air view of Old Melrose, in Roxburghshire, on the south bank of the Tweed, which here makes a loop, almost creating an island. This is the site of the original abbey, about a mile and a half to the east of the town and modern abbey of Melrose. Its founder is unknown, but its first abbot was Eata, followed by Boisil, and then by St Cuthbert. (Cf. p. 149 above.)

67 St Abb's Head, Coldingham, on the Berwickshire coast. The site of an early Celtic monastery, where Aetheldreda, the wife of King Ecgfrith of Northumbria, took the veil before she became abbess of Ely. (Bede, *H.E.* IV, ch. 19; cf. also ch. 25.) The remains of the vallum, covered with earth, and the monastic remains on the edge of the cliff are visible in this air view.